Ignatius Loyola

Christian Mystic

Brian O'Leary SJ

Messenger Publications,
37 Leeson Place, Dublin D02 E5V0
www.messenger.ie

Table of Contents

Preface

Every biography of St Ignatius Loyola includes passages outlining and commenting on his mystical experiences. These incidences can never be omitted – they are integral to his story and are part of who he is. Just as a biographer will deal with his family background and early career as a knight, his conversion and education, and his founding with other companions of the Society of Jesus, so too will his mysticism contribute to the overall portrait. But a biography needs to be comprehensive – Ignatius's mystical experiences will be just one of many focal points.

The present book is not a biography but an enquiry into the mysticism of Ignatius. However, it cannot achieve its aim without setting his mystical experiences in the context of his life. So, some biographical material will be dealt with but only in so far as this is required for the book's purpose.

It will also be necessary to make regular references to the *Spiritual Exercises*.[1] Some readers may already be acquainted with this short book. In it Ignatius outlines a series of meditations and contemplations ('exercises') aimed at facilitating a serious decision in a person's life. Simultaneously, these exercises will help to deepen that person's prayer and bring them closer to God.

It is perhaps surprising that an investigation such as this has not been attempted more often. Apart from translations of monographs in other languages, only one English-language work comes to mind. In 1987 the North American theologian, Harvey Egan SJ, published *Ignatius Loyola the Mystic* as volume 5 in the series

---

1   *The Spiritual Exercises of Saint Ignatius*. A Translation and Commentary by George E. Ganss, SJ Chicago, IL: Loyola University Press, 1992. This translation will be used throughout the book.

'The Way of the Christian Mystics'.[2] Egan's work is still of great value, not least because of his familiarity with the thinking of his mentor, Karl Rahner SJ (1904–1984). My contribution is written in a different style and is intended for a wider readership.

Some may feel – rightly or wrongly – that they don't have sufficient knowledge of the life of Ignatius, or of the *Spiritual Exercises*, to get involved with his mysticism. I have kept such hesitant readers in mind. Accordingly, I outline, as I go along, the background to whatever is happening on the mystical level in Ignatius. Besides, at the first naming of someone in the text, a footnote will give some short biographical information to the reader. I also explain concisely some Ignatian terminology that may be puzzling or potentially misleading.

If all this is not sufficient reassurance, I can recommend *The Pilgrim's Story* by Brendan Comerford SJ as a parallel or complementary text to my own.[3] This relatively short book (166 pages) is helpfully divided into two parts: the first on the life of Ignatius and the second on the *Spiritual Exercises*. This combination provides in a clear and accessible form all the information anyone may need.

Working on this book has constantly brought to mind the many Ignatian scholars from whom I have learned whatever I know. Two stand out from the early years of my interest in studying Ignatian spirituality. They are Gervais Dumeige SJ, who supervised my doctoral studies in Rome (1970–73), and John J. English SJ, who was my tertian instructor in Guelph, Ontario (1975). Their influence is still palpable and formative. My homage to both men, my brother Jesuits.

Among my contemporary friends and colleagues, I want to thank the following for reading individual chapters of this book and providing helpful critiques: Aileen Murphy RLR, Brendan

---

2   Harvey D. Egan, SJ, *Ignatius Loyola the Mystic*. Wilmington, DE: Michael Glazier, 1987. The latest edition comes from the publishers Wipf and Stock, Eugene, OR, 2020.
3   Brendan Comerford SJ, *The Pilgrim's Story: The Life and Spirituality of St Ignatius Loyola*. Dublin: Messenger Publications, 2017.

Comerford SJ, Brendan McManus SJ and Bruce Bradley SJ. Their interest and support have sustained me in times of self-doubt. The quality of the book has been improved through their efforts and they are not responsible for any deficiencies.

Brian O'Leary, SJ

Introduction

For many people the words 'mystic' and 'mysticism' can be simultaneously seductive and scary, conveying both an invitation and a
caveat. This reveals something of the ambiguity of the words but
also their power. Almost all writers on mysticism today – especially
on Christian mysticism – begin by explaining what it is *not*. Or
they at least identify the particular interpretations that they reject
entirely, or will not be addressing. The most widespread agreement
on what needs elimination, or at least bracketing, concerns the
paranormal phenomena associated with mysticism: visions, voices,
ecstasies, stigmata, levitation, bilocation and so forth.

The problem is not with efforts to prove the authenticity of these
experiences – this will always be an open question – but with any
tendency to identify them as the essential core of mysticism. This
they certainly are not. However, despite this cautionary approach,
it must be admitted that such paranormal phenomena are frequently our main point of entry into the experience of the mystics. It is these phenomena that, in many cases, first attract our
attention. They suggest to us that here is something strange and
puzzling, and thus worth exploring. Consequently, even though
we may exclude these phenomena from our core understanding
of mysticism, or bracket them for methodological reasons, they
cannot be ignored completely. We need to ask if they are mediat-
ing something more profound – some presence or influence of the
divine.

Mysticism exists in all faith traditions – those of the East and of
the West. In the nineteenth and twentieth centuries there was a pro-
pensity to go further by claiming that mysticism was essentially
the same in all such traditions. Indeed, mysticism was understood

to be the common element – the golden string – uniting all faiths. There is some truth in this claim. Nevertheless, theologies and philosophies, myths and symbols, sacred texts and rituals of worship, differ significantly across space and time. Hence there will inevitably be differences in the way in which mystical experiences are *received*. Still more will differences be present when mystics attempt to *articulate* and *communicate* their experience. Yet, despite this, the argument goes, the essence of mysticism will always remain constant, unchanging and identifiable as such. Accordingly, it will transcend any contingent ethnic, historical or cultural differences.

In more recent decades there has been a move away from this analysis. Scholars now tend to underline the distinctiveness, even uniqueness of the mysticism found within each tradition. They do not deny the universality of mysticism as a shared human phenomenon. But they affirm that the mystical experiences of figures such as the Christian Teresa of Ávila (1515–1582), the Jew Abraham Abulafia (1240–1291) and the Muslim Abu Hamid al-Ghazali (1058–1111) are *qualitively* different from one another. Each experience is unique – primarily to the individual person – but also to the faith tradition to which that person belongs.

Hence the manifestations of mysticism across the faiths are not simply interchangeable. They do not duplicate one another. Neither are they modulations of the same melody so much as different melodies. Nevertheless, they can be complementary. They have enough in common to interrogate, illuminate, and even interpret one another. The recent history of interfaith dialogue – where the sharing of traditions of prayer and mysticism has turned out to be the most fruitful strand – has shown the truth of these claims.

This book will not be dealing with many of the complicated, even intractable issues touched on above. Its more modest focus will be the mystical experiences of one man – the sixteenth-century Basque priest known as St Ignatius Loyola (1491–1556). We will examine how he describes these experiences, how they affected him, and how they guided him on his life's journey. This will give us the opportunity to reflect on them theologically, seeking to understand them in the light of Christian faith. Our hope is that the reader will also intuit something of the relevance of Ignatius's mysticism for themselves and for the world of today.

Finally, the popular image of the mystic is of a person who is somehow taken out of their own body, or raised above this world. The frequent use of the word 'ecstasy' (Greek *'ekstasis'*) lends itself to this viewpoint. However, the mysticism of Ignatius, far from taking him out of his body or removing him from this world, serves to insert him more firmly into both. This is one of its distinguishing marks.

We have no wish to deny the spiritual, even *supernatural* nature of his mystical gifts. Nevertheless, there is a real sense – even if a highly paradoxical one – in which they can also be called *worldly*. This is a paradox to savour. It can also be expressed by saying that his was an incarnational mysticism, through which *the spirit takes on a body* – his body. This dynamic mirrors the mystery of the Word becoming flesh (John 1:14). The reader is encouraged to keep this tantalising paradox in mind through all that follows.

Chapter i

Christian Mysticism:
Exploring a Tradition

The terms 'mystic' and 'mysticism', now common currency among scholars and lay readers alike, go back only to the seventeenth century. They first began to appear in French Catholic writing in the 1620s and 1630s to refer to the cultivation of the inner life. The seventeenth century was the Golden Age of spirituality in France, and produced what is sometimes known, not entirely satisfactorily, as the French School. Later that century English Quakers were using the terms mystic and mysticism in a similar sense. It is sobering to reflect that, when we refer to someone from the Patristic Age, the Middle Ages, or Early Modern times as a mystic, their contemporaries would have been puzzled, unable to understand what we mean.

How then would Bernard of Clairvaux (1090–1153) or Hildegard of Bingen (1098–1179), for example, be described in their day? They would have been known simply as 'contemplatives'. This fact surprises many people today who are accustomed to calling them mystics. However, it is both enlightening and freeing to recognise that, in the history of Christian terminology, 'contemplation' and 'mysticism' are quasi-synonyms. The mystic is the contemplative; the contemplative is the mystic.

Knowing this is not just a valuable academic insight but one that has pastoral implications. To encourage a person to become a contemplative is somehow less intimidating than to encourage them to become a mystic. Contemplation, while not without its own hint of challenge, is somehow a more unpretentious word – perhaps a more inviting word – than mysticism. It also carries with it less danger of conjuring up the bizarre or the paranormal, which most people rightly shun. Finally, contemplation is a term mostly associated with Christianity – although with Greek philosophical roots. This makes it less likely to be confused with the mysticism of Eastern traditions such as Hinduism and Buddhism, where the term 'meditation' is more likely to be used.

In the interests of simplification, a case can be made for consistently using 'contemplation' instead of 'mysticism', and 'contemplative' instead of 'mystic'. However, this would create its own difficulties and is not really necessary. Indeed, it might not even be possible, since 'mysticism' and 'mystic' are so well established in our current spiritual vocabulary. However, as long as we have become aware of the history of the terms – and remember that in the Christian tradition they are quasi-synonyms – we can work easily with both.

Lectio divina

Many Christians will recognise the term 'contemplation' from their knowledge of *lectio divina*. This way of praying was practised in monastic communities from early in the Christian era. Then it became part of the liturgy celebrated in cathedral churches. It was simple enough to be used by beginners in prayer, yet its inner dynamic could lead a person into a deep consciousness of God. *Lectio divina* was given a new lease of life in the aftermath of the Second Vatican Council. This development was one particular outcome of the new enthusiasm for the study of the Bible, and it has contributed greatly to an evolving lay spirituality. The original monastic model has been creatively adapted to suit the different groups and circumstances in which it is now being practised – especially in parish settings. However, the familiar four steps remained constant: *lectio* (reading), *meditatio* (meditation), *oratio* (prayer), *contemplatio* (contemplation). In what follows we shall mostly concentrate on the third and fourth steps.[4]

---

4   The best presentation of the monastic tradition of *lectio divina* dates from the twelfth century. The author is the Carthusian, Guigo II, the ninth prior of the Grande Chartreuse. An English translation appears in Guigo II, *The Ladder of Monks and Twelve*

In reading and meditation we mull over – ruminate on, like cattle chewing the cud – a chosen passage in the Bible. This engagement with the sacred text already opens us to the enlightenment of the Holy Spirit. We are brought a certain distance on our journey to God. Then, at some point, we find ourselves in what can be called a 'halfway house'. This is a place of rest – a comfort-zone – in whose warmth and solace the thought of settling down may become strangely seductive. An inner voice may be whispering in our ear: 'This is surely far enough! Why travel any further? Isn't this what you were looking for?'

On the other hand, after some time we may feel vaguely discontented or ill at ease – without clearly knowing why. We may sense dimly that there is more on offer further along the road – if we can summon enough courage to continue the journey. A decision is called for. So, after much hesitation and procrastination, we finally resolve to keep moving. This will involve leaving behind the cosiness and security of the halfway house and risking the unknown. All we know is that we are motivated by a desire – however weak and diffident – that we do not understand.

We soon discover – probably to our chagrin – that we are unable to continue the journey by our own efforts. Our desire – whether ardent or timid – is not enough to carry us forward. We feel discouraged, inadequate, vulnerable – maybe a bit fearful. This is holy ground that we are approaching (Exodus 3:5), and we will need some kind of intervention by God to enable us to traverse it. So we reach out – in quiet desperation – for what we know that we cannot obtain by our own efforts. This is the special meaning of *oratio* – a prayer of felt inadequacy, of radical helplessness, of unfulfilled desire.[5]

Sometimes the *oratio* will be uttered wordlessly, simply by holding ourselves before God in an attitude of painful, helpless silence.

Meditations, Kalamazoo, MI: Cistercian Publications, 1981. My reflections are based on this work.

5   Notice that *oratio* in this context does not mean *any* kind of prayer. It is petitionary prayer that is specific to the dynamic of *lectio divina*.

Or it may be articulated through the use of biblical verses such as: 'It is your face, O Lord, that I seek; hide not your face' (Psalm 27:8–9). 'Lord, let us see the Father and then we shall be satisfied' (John 14:8). Such phrases may become mantras, which, by frequent repetition, enable our desires to put down ever-deeper roots within us. We may even feel drawn to pray in the words of the great Spanish Carmelite mystic, St John of the Cross (1542–1591):

> O living flame of love
> that tenderly wounds my soul
> in its deepest centre! Since
> now you are not oppressive,
> now consummate! – if it be your will:
> tear through the veil of this sweet encounter![6]

Contemplatio (contemplation) 'happens' when God graciously responds to our *oratio* – our prayer of desire. God tears through the veil (above) that has not exactly separated us from God, but has blurred our vision of God. We now 'see' in a new way, as though God has come out of hiding and shown himself. We have moved from seeing God in a mirror, dimly, to seeing him face to face (1 Corinthians 13:12). God is with us, and – astonishingly – we know it! All this is pure gift – not the result of trying hard enough, not a reward that we have earned, and certainly not an outcome that we have deserved. Orthodox Christians stress this point by frequently evoking the line of the Psalmist, 'In your light we see light' (Psalm 36:9). In this way they acknowledge and celebrate the total gratuity of *contemplatio*.

More than a method

Today there is a tendency to regard *lectio divina* simply as one method of prayer among others. We recognise that some individuals

---

6 *The Collected Works of St. John of the Cross*, trans. Kieran Kavanaugh OCD and Otilio Rodriguez OCD. Washington, DC: ICS Publications, 1991, 52.

or groups are attracted to it and choose to use it fruitfully. But *lectio divina* can also be understood – indeed must be understood – as the underlying structure of all Christian prayer. This *structure* is present no matter what *method* a person chooses to follow – or even if they claim not to be following any particular method at all. The four components or dimensions – *lectio, meditatio, oratio* and *contemplatio* – are foundational in the prayer of any committed Christian, although a person may not consciously advert to their role or dynamic.

Furthermore, although we speak of *lectio divina* as the underlying structure of prayer, we need not limit this insight to a believer's formal prayer. We can include their multifaceted, faith-imbued life in its entirety – relationships, activities, interests, work and leisure. All of these elements of human life can be – and are meant to be – prayer-full. The New Testament exhorts us more than once to *continual* prayer:

> Rejoice always, pray without ceasing, give thanks in all circumstances; for this is the will of God in Christ Jesus for you. (1 Thessalonians 5:16–18)

> Pray in the Spirit at all times in every prayer and supplication. (Ephesians 6:18)

It is such a prayer-filled life – viewed holistically – that emerges from and enfleshes the spirit and movement that is *lectio divina*. When allowed and encouraged to develop, this movement will lead a person to *contemplatio* – or, if one prefers, to mysticism. Such an outcome is a sign that God is faithful – a theme regularly repeated in the Bible. 'If we are faithless, he remains faithful – for he cannot deny his own self' (2 Timothy 2:13).

It will be helpful to keep this broad understanding of *lectio divina* in mind – as the underlying structure of Christian prayer and Christian living – when reading and interpreting the mystics. This will apply especially to any consideration of the more 'active' mystics, such as Ignatius Loyola.

Mysterium fidei

While the terms 'mystic' and 'mysticism' may be seventeenth-century creations, they are related linguistically to the pre-Christian Greek word *'musterion'* (Latin *'mysterium'*) – rendered in English as 'mystery.' Its basic meaning in ancient Greek (which can be either secular or religious) is that of something hidden or secret. The early Christians were not slow to incorporate this word into their theological vocabulary. It appears twenty-eight times in the New Testament, twenty-one of these being in the Pauline letters. This Christian use of *'musterion'* or 'mystery' can cover a range of meanings that include:

- the dying and rising of Christ (the paschal mystery);
- the life of the sacraments (particularly baptism and Eucharist);
- the bridal relationship between Christ and his Church.

These mysteries are not totally distinct from each other but are interconnected, interwoven. Ultimately they all have their source in the life of the transcendent *musterion* – the hidden and incomprehensible God who is One and Three.

Paul's mission

We might reflect with profit on how Paul uses the word *'musterion'* when he is describing his own mission. In 1 Corinthians 4:1, he describes himself as one of the 'stewards of God's mysteries'. Later, in Colossians 1:25–27, he spells out the intrinsic link between the *musterion* and the mission that he has received from God.

> I became its [the church's] servant according to God's commission that was given to me for you, to make the word of God fully known, the *musterion* that has been hidden throughout the ages and generations but has now been revealed to his saints. To them God chose to make known how great among the Gentiles are the riches of the glory of this *musterion*, which is Christ in you, the hope of glory.

Christian mysticism (as we use the word today) is both Christocentric and – a component that we will see later in Ignatius – Trinitarian. The mystic has a consciousness of 'Christ in you, the hope of glory'. This is not just a notional assent to a creedal statement, but a more or less vivid awareness of the mystery that is the incarnate Word. This consciousness is not limited to an elite but is accessible to all the 'saints' – a favourite Pauline designation for believers. Every Christian has the capacity to become a mystic – or, as earlier centuries would say, a contemplative – provided they do not put major obstacles in the way. Indeed, every Christian *is* a mystic, as long as they allow the mystical consciousness, given at baptism, to awaken and flourish within them. All this is pure gift.

Communal or ecclesial dimension

There is a widespread misapprehension that mysticism belongs exclusively within the private domain of a privileged individual. Its fruits are experienced during solitary prayer, to which the mystic is presumed to devote a great deal of time. Other activities in a mystic's life have to be kept to a minimum so as not to distract from the concentration of all the human faculties on God. This viewpoint contradicts what was stated above about the accessibility of mysticism to all the baptised – most of whom are living ordinary and usually busy lives. They have familial, social and work-related responsibilities that take up most of their time and energy. But what if there could be a mysticism in the midst of the world or, as some call it, an everyday mysticism? This is in fact what those in today's Ignatian circles refer to as 'finding God in all things'.

Furthermore, the 'great' mystics – whose writings are revered, and whose legacy lives on – did not spring up out of nowhere. They had first to be nurtured and nourished in the living faith of a Christian community. They participated in its corporate worship, received its sacraments, contributed to its prophetic witness, and rejoiced in its self-awareness as the body of Christ – the Mystical

Body. To speak of them as 'great' is not to label them as totally different from the rest of us, as though they lived in some kind of parallel universe. We all belong to the one body.

> For just as the body is one and has many members, and all the members of the body, though many, are one body, so it is with Christ ... Now you are the body of Christ and individually members of it. (1 Corinthians 12:12, 27)

Imagine a vast mountain range as a symbol for the totality of Christian believers. It rises from the valleys, and its foothills are initially quite modest in height. Their slopes climb almost imperceptibly until – sometimes abruptly, sometimes more gradually – mountains begin to appear. This brings about a dramatic change in the landscape. These mountains vary greatly in height. But among them, some few soar majestically upwards until their peaks become snow-clad before disappearing into the clouds. They are breathtaking and mysterious, evoking our sense of wonder and awe. Yet even these highest mountains do not stand alone. They would not even be in existence were they not conjoined with the other mountains – and even with the foothills. All are part of the one range. All are interconnected and interdependent. So it is with the great mystics and the people of God.

Von Hügel and Julian of Norwich
Baron Friedrich von Hügel (1852–1925), an Austrian lay theologian and apologist, wrote an influential book called *The Mystical Element of Religion*.[7] He argued that the Church must encompass three essential elements: historical-institutional, intellectual-speculative and mystical-experiential. If any of these elements are absent, or underdeveloped, the necessary balance within the Church is lost. It follows that mysticism is never an optional

---

7 Friedrich von Hügel, *The Mystical Element of Religion as Studied in Saint Catherine of Genoa and her Friends*. Aeterna Press, 1909/2015.

extra – icing on the cake, as it were. The enlivening presence of mysticism – that of the 'greats' and that of ordinary believers – is essential for the Church's well-being. Without it the Church loses its God-centredness, fails to witness effectively, and lacks the inner fire needed for mission. It will soon be no more than a well-meaning NGO. The salt will have lost its taste; the light will be dimmed, if not extinguished (see Matthew 5:13–16).

A valid question arises when we shift our attention from the impact of mysticism – or mystics in general – on the Church to that of the individual mystic. How does such a person exercise influence? Is it sufficient for the mystic simply to exist and act like leaven in the dough (Luke 13:20–21)? Does the anonymous (and silent) mystic fulfil their calling and exercise their influence in spite of – or even by means of – their very hiddenness? It would be foolhardy to rule out such a proposition entirely. God works in an infinite variety of ways. However, many mystics have felt a responsibility to communicate something of what they have experienced to the wider community. Their mystical experiences are not meant to be hoarded as a miser hoards a treasure.

The English mystic, Julian of Norwich (1342– after 1416), certainly wanted her voice to be heard, although she was living the life of a recluse. She situates this desire precisely in the context of the communal nature of the Church. After describing one of her early 'showings' (visions), she writes:

> For it [the showing] is universal and addressed to all because we are all one, and I am sure I saw it for the advantage of many others. Indeed, it was not shown to me because God loved me better than the lowest soul that is in the state of grace, for I am sure that there are very many who never had a showing or vision ... and who love God better than I do. For if I look solely at myself, I am really nothing; but as one of mankind in general, I am in oneness of love with all my fellow-Christians; for upon this oneness of love depends the life of all who shall be saved; for

God is all that is good, and God has made all that is made, and God loves all that he has made.[8]

Julian speaks simply and clearly, with an admirable mix of confidence and humility. Her central point in the above quotation – that her showings or visions are not meant for herself alone – validates the study, not only of Julian herself, but of all the mystics who have left us their testimony. As a general principle, their experiences of God – while remaining uniquely their own – contain revelation, enlightenment and consolation for all believers. We are encouraged not just to learn *about* the mystics but to learn *from* them. They can accompany, guide and nourish us in our own search for God.

A similar teaching is found in the medieval Dominican theologian, Thomas Aquinas (1225–1274). He wrote, 'For even as it is better to enlighten than merely to shine, so it is better to give to others what one has contemplated than merely to contemplate.'[9] This led to the well-known Dominican motto: *Contemplari et contemplata aliis tradere*, which can be paraphrased as: To contemplate and to hand on to others – to share with others – the fruits of our contemplation. This again shows an awareness of all being members of the one body – the Church – in which we each nourish the other through our unique giftedness. 'No man is an island entire of itself', as John Donne (1572–1631) wrote so succinctly, yet so tellingly.

Ignatius of Loyola

With all this in mind, we turn to the well-known yet frequently misunderstood figure of Ignatius of Loyola (1491–1556), founder of the Society of Jesus (Jesuits). In more recent years he has come to be recognised – at least by those who have seen beyond the stereotypes – as a remarkable mystic. The culture and lifestyle of

8 Julian of Norwich, *Revelations of Divine Love*, trans. Elizabeth Spearing, London: Penguin Classics, 1998, 10. [Short Text ch.6].
9 *Summa Theologiae*, II–II. 188.6.

Julian and Ignatius could hardly have been more different. Walled up in her cell, the English recluse had minimum contact with the outside world. She chose to be part of the eremitical tradition that reached back to the Fathers and Mothers of the Desert in the early centuries of the Church. Ignatius, the Basque nobleman, lived at the throbbing centre of the Renaissance world, immersed in its concerns and competing ideologies. Both during his younger years in Spain as a *caballero* and courtier – we think of his extravagant heroics during the siege of Pamplona – and during his later years in Rome as a priest and Superior General of the Jesuits, he was a man of action. He always wanted to influence events, to shape history.

The sixteenth century was the era when Renaissance humanism had become the dominant culture throughout Europe. It had replaced medieval scholasticism, which had been in decline since its high point in the thirteenth century. This was also the age of a series of religious reformations, both Catholic and Protestant. As these unfolded, the activists on each side, clerical and lay, displayed a mixture of high ideals and an inability or unwillingness to compromise. The sad outcome was a fractured Church and, eventually, the wars of religion that devastated seventeenth-century Europe.

By any standards Ignatius lived in a time of radical change and constant turmoil – in politics, culture and Church life. Being a man of sensibility and intelligence, he found this world and its anxieties present and active within his own soul. Through their tortuous intricacies he sought to find his way – and God's will – by means of spiritual discernment. He refused to hide or escape – he needed to be involved. To carry out this project the contemplative and active dimensions of his personality had to develop in tandem. He is often called a *pilgrim* – a term used frequently in the *Autobiography* – but, more importantly, he was a *searcher* and a *doer*. All of this is the backdrop to be kept in mind as we explore his unique brand of mysticism.

Spiritual senses

As already indicated, this is not an academic book, so there will be little discussion of the more speculative questions regarding mysticism. Most of the chapters (3–6) will simply describe and reflect on actual experiences of God as recorded by Ignatius himself or by those closest to him. However, in offering an interpretation of these experiences, it will be necessary from time to time to call on some well-established theological insights. These will be woven into the narrative and should be readily understandable in their context. Nevertheless, it may be helpful to draw attention to one particular strand in the Christian tradition so that we remain alert to it throughout our reading. I refer to the teaching on the *spiritual senses*.[10]

Since the time of Aristotle it has been generally accepted that we possess five physical senses – sight, hearing, smell, taste and touch. Later, Christian writers on prayer and mysticism began to teach that we also have five spiritual or inner senses to which the same terms can be applied. Just as the physical senses allow us to connect with – have a relationship with – the material world, so the spiritual senses allow us to connect with – have a relationship with – the world of the divine.

Such linguistic usage can already be found throughout Scripture – as when the psalmist longs to *see* the face of God (Psalm 27:8), or the prophets exhort us to *hear* the word of the Lord (Isaiah 1:10), or we are encouraged to *taste* (and see) that the Lord is good (Psalm 34:8), or when Paul speaks of believers being the *sweet aroma* of Christ (2 Corinthians 2:15), or the Johannine witnesses to the resurrection claim to have *touched* with their own hands the Word of Life (1 John 1:1).

The term '*spiritual senses*' is first found in the Latin translation of the works of Origen of Alexandria (185–254), was explored by

---

10 *The Spiritual Senses: Perceiving God in Western Christianity*, Paul L. Gavrilyuk and Sarah Coakley (eds), Cambridge: Cambridge University Press, 2012.

major figures such as St Augustine (354–430), St Gregory the Great (c.540–604), and the Venerable Bede (c.673–735), and has endured with varying nuances and interpretations to the present day. The subtleties of this tradition, and the philosophical arguments underpinning it, need not concern us. What is more important is to notice how often this manner of speaking occurs in authors exploring the spiritual life, and indeed how often we ourselves use it almost unwittingly. Even in non-religious usage, we speak of the senses being the gateway to the soul – not quite the same idea but related.

Ignatius repeatedly uses sense language in the *Spiritual Exercises*, arguably as a way of facilitating simplicity and immediacy in a person's prayer. Indeed, he even composes an exercise called 'an application of the five senses' (121–126; also 65–71). This prayer begins with a deliberate use of our imagination to see, hear, smell, taste and touch the entire scenario of a gospel scene – persons in their interrelationships, conversations taking place, actions being performed, and even the physical location. The hope is that this *active* beginning – using our imaginative senses – will awaken and stir into life the spiritual senses. These will then draw us ever more deeply into a *passive* – even mystical – appreciation of the scene being contemplated and the persons present in it.

When Ignatius was Superior General, Antonio Brandão, a young Portuguese Jesuit, sent him a number of questions about prayer. He was having difficulties in this area due to the pressure of his studies. Ignatius's long reply includes an interesting reference to praying with the senses (my emphases):

> In view of the end of our studies, the scholastics cannot engage in long meditations ... [However], they can practise seeking the presence of our Lord in all things: in their dealings with other people, their walking, *seeing, tasting, hearing*, understanding, and all our activities ... This kind of meditation – finding God our Lord in everything – is

easier than lifting ourselves up and laboriously making ourselves present to more abstracted divine realities.[11]

Ignatius also uses sense language in describing his own mystical experiences. This does not imply that these experiences are merely sensual. Indeed, he will at times underline the fact that this is *not* so. However, this sense language indicates both that the spiritual senses had been awakened in Ignatius and that he often finds it the best way of communicating what he had experienced. Consequently, if readers are attentive to his use of the language of the senses, they will be opening up for themselves a relatively easy way of entering into his experience of God.[12]

---

11 *Ignatius of Loyola: Letters and Instructions*, trans. Martin E. Palmer SJ, John W. Padberg SJ, John L. McCarthy SJ. St Louis, MO: Institute of Jesuit Sources, 2006, 342.
12 Further reading: Timothy W. O'Brien SJ, '*Con Ojos Interiores*: Ignatius of Loyola and the Spiritual Senses'. *Studies in Spirituality* 26 (2016), 263–81.

Chapter 2

The *Autobiography*: Our First Resource

Did Ignatius believe that his mystical experiences were meant for him alone, or did he feel any obligation to share them with others? There is no simple answer to this question. There were times when he spoke quite openly, even spontaneously, about the visions he was receiving and the joy that accompanied them. At other times he was reluctant to do so, or was conflicted by his inability to see clearly where the will of God lay in the matter. His circumstances – the context of his visions – changed as his life unfolded. The visions themselves took on differences in content and form. It is not surprising that the question – to share or not to share? – raised different issues at each stage of his journey. Some of this complexity is illustrated in the genesis of the text we know as the *Autobiography*.[13] This is one reason for devoting a chapter to examining this work in some detail. We will see that the very existence of the *Autobiography* is the outcome of a protracted inner struggle around this very question.

Background and image

Over the centuries since 1556, the year of his death, Ignatius has been interpreted through a variety of images. The most conspicuous and constant image for most of this period was that of the soldier-saint. This image drew partly on Ignatius's patrimony in the bellicose minor aristocracy of the Basque country. Linked with this was his upbringing in the chivalric culture of the day,

---

13 *A Pilgrim's Journey: The Autobiography of Ignatius of Loyola*. A translation and commentary by Joseph N. Tylends, SJ. San Francisco, CA: Ignatius Press (revised edition 2001). This translation will be used throughout this book.

which included training in the art of warfare. Then there was the siege of Pamplona (1521) and his flamboyant, though foolhardy, exploits there. However, the image also drew on an understanding of the Society of Jesus as an organisation, structured like an army, and founded with the specific intention of destroying Luther and the Protestant Reformation. Although historically untrue, this narrative was commonly accepted in both Catholic and Protestant circles alike – evoking admiration and vituperation in equal measure.

Shortly after the Second Vatican Council the image of Ignatius the pilgrim began to gain traction and to increase in popularity. Indeed, it has replaced the soldier-saint as the dominant image ever since. The chief reason for this development has been the rediscovery of, and the widespread attention given to the *Autobiography*. In this text Ignatius is called a pilgrim no fewer than eighty-five times! Readers believed that this was a self-designation by Ignatius himself – although this is questionable.[14] However, the image of the pilgrim has many attractions for people, as it gives Ignatius a more human face and makes him seem less in control and less intimidating. It conveys a sense of ordinariness and simplicity – of someone searching for their true self and for God.

Then there is Ignatius the mystic – the subject of this book. The wholehearted embrace of this image is even more recent – perhaps from the turn of the millennium. Again, it has its source in the *Autobiography*, although, as we will see, its deepest roots lie in the less well known *Spiritual Diary* (see Chapter 6). Note that the image of Ignatius the mystic has not replaced that of Ignatius the pilgrim. Indeed, the two images are regarded as complementing each other – it is even possible to speak of the pilgrim-mystic. It is also worth observing that this growth of interest in Ignatius as

---

14 It is more likely that the designation 'pilgrim' is a literary construct by Luis Gonçalves da Câmara, the Jesuit to whom Ignatius dictated his memoirs. See footnote 19.

a mystic is taking place at a time when there is a greater curiosity about mysticism in the wider culture.

'Tell me a story'

One of the most productive developments in modern-day theology and spirituality is an appreciation of *story* or *narrative* as a source or a carrier of revelation. We value in a special way the story-telling of the Old Testament, along with that of the Gospels and other New Testament writings. However, we also appreciate those later stories of the holy men and women that permeate the Christian tradition. Increasingly, contemporary searchers for God are finding in story an accessible and engaging way of learning about the mysterious interaction of God with God's people.

Stories have the capacity to illuminate and instruct not by communicating truth in an abstract or purely rational way but by persuading the searcher to enter imaginatively into another's story. This then brings to a heightened awareness the searcher's own story through their recognition of parallels and similarities, and most of all through affective resonances, whether joyful or painful.

Some scholars hold that most of what we know has come to us through stories. Afterwards, partly because it is impossible to remember so many stories over a lifetime, we compress these stories into rational insights and ideas that are easier to store in our memory. When our turn comes to teach others, we tend first to make use of these insights and ideas rather than narrate the original stories which we may have forgotten. However, when, as often happens, our students experience difficulties in comprehending, we may be forced to create new stories that will make the truths in question more communicable – even more appealing.

Spiritual autobiography

For all these reasons we find a growing interest in that genre of writing that is regularly called 'spiritual autobiography'. There is no doubt that this is a suitable term. However, it may run the risk of associating such writings too closely with the 'secular' auto-biographies of politicians, explorers, sports stars, cultural icons etc. This can be seriously misleading. Secular autobiography deals with what a particular person (the author) has experienced in life, aimed at, achieved, thought and said. The narrative revolves around the author.

Spiritual autobiography, in contrast, deals with how God has revealed Godself in and through the author's life. It is the record of what God has been doing and what God has 'achieved'. God is the real protagonist, the central character in the story. Of course, the author's actions and reactions, thoughts and feelings are also recorded. Most importantly, the author's human freedom is seen to be continuously in play – God respects the laws of his own creation. But the author portrays and interprets this human dimension in terms of the initiative of God who is ubiquitously present and active.

In the Christian tradition spiritual autobiography can be said to begin with Paul's account of his conversion – first in Galatians 1:11–24, and later in Acts 22:3–21 and 26:9–20. From these brief early prototypes the genre grew, embracing many and varied forms according to the personality, motivation, objective and literary ability of the narrator. Three principal sub-divisions of the genre emerged:

- The *spiritual autobiography* properly so-called. This is when a person sets out intentionally to recount the spiritual or religious experiences – sometimes mystical – of a longer or shorter period of their life.
- The *spiritual journal* in which the writer records – sometimes on a day-by-day basis – incidents, impressions, feelings, moods, thoughts etc. that relate to their search for God or their experience of God. What is recorded may have occurred at any time or in any circumstance, although they are usually associated – directly or indirectly – with the person's prayer.

- *Letters* in which the writer shares what has been going on within them in their relationship with God. There may be one or more recipients in mind. If these are close friends, the sharing may well be mutual. Alternatively, the recipient may be the writer's spiritual director, and the letter takes the place of a face-to-face meeting. Or – if deemed potentially helpful – the recipient may be a person to whom the writer gives spiritual direction or guidance.

Light from the *Spiritual Exercises*

The *Spiritual Exercises* ends with the Contemplation to Attain the Love of God (230–237). The content and dynamic of this prayer-exercise enable us to grasp what makes spiritual autobiography possible. On entering into this contemplation, I (the retreatant) encounter a God who showers his gifts and blessings on me, and who desires, as far as he can, to give himself to me (First Point); a God who dwells in all creatures, including me, indeed who makes a temple of me (Second Point); a God who labours for me in all creatures, and who labours in me for all creatures (Third Point); a God who is the source of all human goodness and virtue, and who allows me to participate in his own goodness and virtue (Fourth Point).

In theological language, Ignatius presents in this prayer-exercise – especially in its Second and Third Points – an *immanent* God. Such a God is discovered and encountered *within* human experience rather than *beyond* (or transcending) it.[15] This is the God of the Incarnation – Word becoming flesh – and of history. It follows that, since God is so deeply immersed in his own creation, God's story is intimately interwoven with our human story. Consequently, each of us is able to tell, not only our own story, but that part of God's story that has become uniquely ours. This is spiritual

---

15 God is both immanent *and* transcendent – so to affirm one reality is not to deny the other.

autobiography – made possible precisely because of God's imma-
nence in each of us individually, and in all of God's creation.

The *Autobiography* of Ignatius

The Second Vatican Council mandated that all religious orders
return to the sources (*ad fontes*) of their tradition.[16] Since then,
Jesuits and others have given great attention to the text popularly
known in English as the *Autobiography*. It was originally known
simply as *Acta Patris Ignatii* (the Acts of Father Ignatius) – a title
almost certainly meant to evoke the New Testament's *Acta Apos-
tolorum*. This document purports to be a first-hand account by the
saint himself of his life from 1521 (when he was wounded during
the siege of Pamplona) to 1538 (the year after his ordination to
the priesthood and arrival in Rome with the first companions).
As we saw above, the study of this work has been the greatest
influence in changing the dominant image of Ignatius from the
soldier-saint to the pilgrim-mystic. The *Autobiography* is a short
book, relatively easy to read, and hence has become more popular
that many longer biographies and studies.

The genesis of the *Autobiography* is explained in the Preface written by Jerónimo Nadal,[17] a close confidant of Ignatius. In 1553
he had been entrusted with the task of expounding the recently
completed Constitutions to Jesuit communities in Portugal and
Spain. But on these visits he found that he was also asked to speak
about Ignatius himself. The Society had been expanding rapidly
and most Jesuits had never met their Superior General. They
wanted to know more about him. What was Nadal to say? If only
he could successfully persuade Ignatius to be more forthcoming
about his life and experiences! However, he and other Jesuits had
been trying and failing in this endeavour for some time.

---

16 *Perfectae Caritatis* – Decree on the Up-to-date Renewal of Religious Life (1965), par. 2.
17 Jerónimo Nadal (1507–1580) was born in Palma de Mallorca. He became a priest and
    enjoyed a distinguished ecclesiastical and academic career. After a long, difficult dis-
    cernment he entered the Society of Jesus in 1545. Apart from Ignatius himself, Nadal
    exercised the greatest influence on the emerging self-identity and ethos of the Society
    in the sixteenth century. His name will appear frequently in these pages.

Ignatius was not opposed in principle to his companions knowing about his experiences – even those of a mystical nature. However, he preferred to communicate orally – mainly to individuals – especially when he saw that such sharing would benefit the hearer(s). This motivation lessened the possibility of his falling into vainglory – always his most persistent temptation. But to turn these informal conversations into a published text that would be disseminated around the world – would that be a step too far? Could he undertake such a project without serious risk of vainglory? This scruple was the main source of resistance that Nadal continued to encounter as he tried to get Ignatius to change his mind.

Nadal was acutely aware that time was not on his side. Ignatius was in bad health and it was acknowledged that he could die at any time. In his Preface to the *Acta* Nadal recounts that one day in August 1551 (although more likely it was 1552),[18] during a conversation between the two men, Ignatius said to him, 'Just now I was higher than heaven'. Nadal interpreted this enigmatic statement as referring to an ecstasy or rapture and, out of an understandable curiosity, he asked: 'Father, what do you mean?' But Ignatius evaded the question by changing the conversation. Nadal continues:

> Thinking that this was the suitable moment, I begged the Father to be kind enough to tell us how the Lord had guided him from the beginning of his conversion, so that his explanation could serve us as a testament and paternal instruction. Thus, I said to him: 'Since God has granted you the three graces you desired before your death, we fear, Father, that you will soon be called to heaven.'

---

18 Nadal wrote his Preface some time between 1561 and 1576. This lapse of time since the original text was composed (1553–55) may explain some inaccuracies in the text around dates.

The graces to which Nadal was referring were the Pope's confirmation of the Institute of the Society; the parallel confirmation of the *Spiritual Exercises*; and Ignatius's completion of the Constitutions. These goals had all been reached in 1540, 1548 and 1550 respectively. It is as though Nadal, somewhat insensitively, is telling Ignatius that he has nothing further to live for! In any case, his message is clear: Ignatius has little time left on this earth, so he had better tell his story while he can – *now*! Procrastination would benefit nobody. However, despite the force of Nadal's arguments, nothing tangible emerged from this conversation.

In 1553, when Nadal returned to Rome after a period spent in Sicily, he asked Ignatius if he had done anything about his earlier request. Ignatius replied: 'Nothing'! The following year again (this time after returning from Spain) Nadal asked Ignatius the same question and got a similar reply. Becoming more and more exasperated, Nadal thought of a different approach. His Preface reads:

> I do not know what impelled me, but I insisted with the Father: 'It is now going on four years that not only have I asked you, but also other fathers, for you to explain to us, Father, how the Lord had formed you from the beginning of your conversion; for we are confident that knowing this would be most beneficial to us and to the Society. But since I see that you will not grant it to us, I dare to make this statement: If you grant this request we so earnestly desire, we will put it to our best use, and if you do not grant it, our spirits will not be thereby dejected, but we will have the same confidence in the Lord as if you had written everything down.

In this conversation Nadal is expressing *indifference* as to whether Ignatius agrees to tell his story or not. He, and the other Jesuits, will accept Ignatius's decision and be at peace with it. In the *Spiritual Exercises* the notion of indifference plays a key role. The word does not have our contemporary meaning of apathy or lack of interest, but denotes a deep-seated inner freedom in the face of alternative eventualities or possible options. The Principle and Foundation at the beginning of the *Exercises* includes the statement:

> Consequently, on our own part we ought not to seek health rather than sickness, wealth rather than poverty, honour rather than dishonour, a long life rather than a short one, and so on in all other matters. (23)

The expression of indifference on Nadal's part was probably genuine – arrived at over the four years during which he saw his project repeatedly deferred by Ignatius. On the other hand, a reader of a more sceptical bent might be tempted to see Nadal as being cleverly manipulative. However that may be, having failed so often with a frontal assault, Nadal's new, more oblique approach disarmed Ignatius. He no longer felt that he was being pressurised, even bulldozed, into complying with what Nadal (and others) wanted. Nadal's expression of indifference created for Ignatius a space within which he could discern more freely – without feeling coerced. In this more serene atmosphere he could face his fear of vainglory, and weigh up the benefits that would accrue from acquiescing to Nadal's request. That very day, if Nadal's memory is correct on this point, Ignatius began to tell his story.

This background to the emergence of the *Autobiography* alerts us to two key factors that we do well to keep in mind:

• What Ignatius was being asked for was not his life story as such – autobiography as the word is understood today – but an account of *how God had led him since the beginning of his conversion*. In other words, it was to be spiritual autobiography in the strict sense – with God as the main protagonist. As such, the narrative would inevitably include his mystical experiences.

• Nadal was convinced that God was leading the Society of Jesus as a body – and all its individual members – in the same way as God had led Ignatius. Hence, if Ignatius told his story in the way requested by Nadal – focused on how God had led him – this would be enormously beneficial to all Jesuits. It would serve as a prototype or paradigm for their own lives, and would offer them both enlightenment and encouragement. This conviction of Nadal's – which became one of his favourite themes and central to his understanding of Jesuit identity – still has a strong influence on Jesuits today.

Da Câmara's Account

The *Autobiography* has a second Preface, composed by the Jesuit to whom Ignatius chose to narrate (dictate) his story, Luís Gonçalves da Câmara.[19] This Preface was written considerably earlier than Nadal's – it accompanied the original publication of the *Acta*. Unsurprisingly, it provides a different perspective from that of Nadal and it has a different purpose. The two Prefaces complement each other.

One day in August 1553 Ignatius and da Câmara were speaking in the garden of the Roman house. The latter was sharing what was going on in his soul and he described to Ignatius how difficult he found overcoming his tendency to vainglory. In reply, Ignatius, by way of reassurance, revealed his own struggles in this area and how eventually he had reached an inner peace. Da Câmara continues:

An hour or two later we were at dinner, and while Master Polanco[20] and I were eating with him, our Father said that

19 Luís Gonçalves da Câmara (1520–1575) was a Portuguese Jesuit who was sent to Rome after making his final vows in 1553. Apart from his role in the composition of the *Autobiography*, he also wrote a *Memoriale*, in which he recorded the daily life of Ignatius in Rome. See *Remembering Iñigo: Glimpses of the Life of Saint Ignatius of Loyola. The* Memoriale *of Luís Gonçalves da Câmara*. Translated with introduction, notes and indices by Alexander Eaglestone and Joseph A. Munitiz SJ. St Louis, MO: Institute of Jesuit Sources, 2004. Henceforth *Remembering Iñigo*.
20 Juan Alfonso de Polanco (1517–1576), a Spanish Jesuit from Burgos, served as secretary to Ignatius from 1547–56. He collaborated closely with Ignatius in the writing of the *Constitutions*.

many times Master Nadal and others of the Society had made a special request of him, but he had never come to any decision about it. Now, after having spoken with me, and having gone to his room, he felt a powerful inclination and desire to fulfil that request, and – speaking in such a way that it was clear that God had inspired him to see what his duty was – was now determined to do it, that is, narrate all that had happened in his soul up to the present time, and he likewise decided that I was to be the one to whom he would reveal these matters.

The conversation in the garden had changed something in Ignatius – and had done so quite suddenly and unexpectedly. When he came to dinner not long afterwards and broached the hitherto thorny subject of Nadal's request, he made no mention of his fear of vainglory. This no longer had a hold over him. He seemed to be speaking from some newly attained place of inner freedom. It was as if his fear had been purged through his listening to, and engaging with another human being who suffered from the same temptation. The conversation had been therapeutic and liberating for both Ignatius and da Câmara.

However, something else was missing from what Ignatius was saying at the dinner table. He made no reference to the justifications that he had regularly given over recent years for putting the project, requested by Nadal, on indefinite hold – ill health, burdens of governance, apostolic commitments and so forth. He was now able to ignore these excuses too. In retrospect, he probably saw his earlier appeals to them as false reasonings suggested by an evil spirit.

Now he felt inspired by God and had been given 'a powerful inclination and desire to fulfil that request'. This brought his resistances to an abrupt end. Fear had been overcome by desire – indeed a powerful desire *given by God* – so he would certainly do as he was asked. And he would do so, not because of the importunity of Nadal and others, but because he now realised that this was what God wanted him to do. God's desire had become his desire – and that desire was abundantly clear. Finally, this coming together of the two desires – his own and God's – left him in consolation. Out of this consolation – with its peace, light and joy – he would tell his story, and da Câmara, much to his surprise, would be its designated recipient.[21]

Résumé

Every mystic is faced with the question: 'To share or not to share?' It is remarkable how difficult Ignatius found it to come to a satisfactory answer in his own case. Notice, however, that there is always an accompanying subsidiary question: 'How to share?' It was this second question that caused him the most uncertainty. Whenever he was asked by Nadal to tell his story, he never refused outright – he procrastinated. He had no objection to sharing with others how God had led him – even to recounting his mystical experiences – when he thought that this would benefit others, but he baulked at the format that Nadal had in mind, and particularly at the prospect of such a narrative's wide dissemination. This would not be the intimate face-to-face sharing with which he was comfortable, but self-exposure to an unseen and unknown global readership. Here was the greatest stumbling block, and ignoring it would surely lead him into vainglory.

Our surprise at this indecisiveness may be compounded by the clarity and assurance of Ignatius's teaching on discernment in the *Spiritual Exercises*. To this can be added his acknowledged skills in helping other people who were facing a serious choice in their lives. However, as experienced spiritual directors will concede, it

---

21 This decision of Ignatius, not to write anything himself but to dictate his story, led to the following sequence repeating itself a number of times: i) Ignatius dictates part of his story; ii) Da Câmara listens in silence without taking notes; iii) Da Câmara retires and makes a summary of what he has heard; iv) He later expands these notes into a fuller version; v) He dictates this fuller version to a scribe. This complex procedure raises many questions: Whose voice are we hearing? Who is the 'author' of the final text? etc.

is easier to master the theory of discernment – even to apply it to others – than to deal with problematic issues arising in one's own life. Even in his later years Ignatius was not immune from inner resistances, or from the confusion that results from them. His mysticism did not guarantee him a shortcut to certainty.

The genesis of the *Autobiography* – described in the two Prefaces – shows why it is our first resource for learning about Ignatius's mystical experiences. In it he was answering Nadal's question about how God had led him since his conversion. God had enlightened, guided and encouraged him in a variety of ways – some were mystical, others more ordinary. Both are recorded in the *Autobiography* – as are the changing contexts in which they occur. In some instances, Ignatius's version of what he had experienced is confirmed – or even expanded on – by one or other of his early companions. We will include some of their statements.

As we read the *Autobiography*, we will need to keep in mind that it was dictated many years after the happenings that it records. The narrative begins in 1521 and ends in 1538, whereas the dictation on which it is based took place from 1553 to 1555. Ignatius's account is essentially a retrospective one. It is shot through with the ambiguities of selective memory, and the obscurities – as well as the wisdom – of hindsight.

An ongoing question for us might be: Is Ignatius here describing how he understands and feels about these events *now* (in Rome), or how he understood and felt about them *then* (whenever and wherever they occurred)? The plain, even terse style of the *Autobiography* can give the impression of a clarity in Ignatius's mind that was not necessarily his at the time of the actual events.

The Roman Ignatius had certainly reached a greater spiritual maturity than that of the callow younger man convalescing in Loyola, or agonising over the meaning of his life in Manresa. From the point of view of telling his story, however, this can be seen both as an advantage and a disadvantage. It is good for readers of the *Autobiography* to be at least aware of this difficulty. Such awareness will make us more vigilant as we enter empathetically – though not naively – into his narrative.

CHAPTER 3

Early Mystical Experiences:
Loyola and Manresa

After being wounded while defending the citadel of Pamplona against a French army in 1521, Ignatius had been brought to the family home at Loyola in the Basque country. He needed time to recover and build up his strength following painful surgery. The first remarkable spiritual event recorded in the *Autobiography* took place during this period of convalescence. From his reading of the *Vita Christi* (*Life of Christ*) by Ludolph of Saxony,[22] and the *Flos Sanctorum* (or the *Golden Legend* – a collection of lives of the saints) by Jacobus de Voragine,[23] – the only books available to him – his worldview and ideals had gradually changed. Up to now they had been those of an ambitious knight, embodying the culture of chivalry and serving an earthly king. Now his ideals and desires were morphing into those of a penitent – a poor pilgrim serving Christ, the heavenly king. His reading offered him multiple examples of how Gospel values had been lived out – firstly by Christ – and then by faith-filled men and women throughout history. These exemplars became his 'great cloud of witnesses' (Hebrews 12:1), feeding into and guiding his ruminations on his own life and future.

In the *Autobiography* (7) Ignatius picks out Francis and Dominic for special mention. They are saints whom he not only greatly admires but wishes to emulate. He goes so far as to say to himself: 'Saint Dominic did this, so I have to do it too. Saint Francis did this, so I have to do it too.' What he most concentrates on are the

22 Ludolph of Saxony (1300–1377), German Carthusian theologian.
23 Jacobus de Voragine (1228–1298), Italian Dominican, Bishop of Genoa.

heroics of their self-abnegation, penances and austerities. He was not sufficiently spiritually mature to recognise their inner virtues (such as humility). Ignatius was still the product of his chivalric training, which had prepared knights for a life devoted to *great deeds*. These would ensure recognition, honour and glory. This deeply ingrained ethos continued to play a seminal role throughout his conversion. Loyola was only a first stage, an initial transformation. Ignatius recalls one important turning point:

> With these holy desires of his, the thoughts of his former life were soon forgotten and this was confirmed by a vision in this manner. One night, as he lay sleepless, he clearly saw the likeness of our Lady with the holy Child Jesus, and because of this vision he enjoyed an excess of consolation for a remarkably long time. He felt so great a loathsomeness for all his past life, especially for the deeds of the flesh, that it seemed to him that all the images that had been previously imprinted on his mind were now erased. Thus from that hour until August 1553, when this is being written, he never again consented, not even in the least matter, to the motions of the flesh. (10)

While Ignatius here highlights his sexual sins, we note that it is for his whole former lifestyle that he expresses loathing and disgust. Promiscuous behaviour was a part of that lifestyle but it also symbolises *all* the false values that had deceived and ruled him. Hence, the release brought by this vision of Our Lady and the Child Jesus from temptations against chastity also unburdens him of other unhealthy desires and obsessions. He begins to enjoy a freedom to choose higher goals and a more satisfying mode of living – with God now at the centre of his world.

Ignatius goes on to say that 'because of this effect on him he concluded that this had been God's doing'. The authenticity of the vision – and of the 'excess of consolation' that accompanied it – was confirmed by the positive change that it brought about in him. Thus, at this early stage of his conversion, Ignatius is already applying a criterion found in the Christian tradition for the discernment of spirits. It had been articulated by Jesus in the New Testament – 'You will know them by their fruits' (Matthew 7:16). As Ignatius had no religious formation of any depth, and no spiritual director at the time, it is likely that he learned this criterion from his perusal of the *Vita Christi* and *Flos Sanctorum*.

Five lessons

It is in the following year (1522), during an eleven-month sojourn in the town of Manresa, that Ignatius receives more frequent and more significant mystical experiences. These are also more difficult to interpret. However, before coming to these experiences, the *Autobiography* has a long description of his battles with scruples, so intense and soul-destroying that he came close to suicide (22–25). This is followed by a passage of apparent simplicity, yet of great substance, in which he records:

> During this period God was dealing with him in the same way a schoolteacher deals with a child while instructing him. This was because either he was thick and dull of brain, or because of the firm will that God Himself had implanted in him to serve Him – but he clearly recognized and has always recognized that it was in this way that God dealt with him. Furthermore, if he were to doubt this, he would think he was offending the Divine Majesty. One can see how God dealt with him in the following five examples. (27)

Having led Ignatius through the excruciating saga of his scruples, God now offers him further lessons – five of which Ignatius has chosen to share with us. These 'lessons' will be of a different kind. They will not aim at helping Ignatius to solve some tortuous case of conscience – some moral issue that confounds him. Their purpose will be to enlighten him on the central themes of Christian faith. These lessons will not constitute a theodicy (a course of

43

studies on natural theology), but rather a mystagogy (an induction of Ignatius into the great Mystery at the heart of the universe).

The sequence begins with a vision of the Trinity, followed by an insight into how God created the world. Then comes an understanding of how Christ is present in the Eucharist. Next, the humanity of Christ and Our Lady show themselves to him. He treats these two visions as one – presumably because of their similarity of form. Finally comes the 'great enlightenment' on the banks of the River Cardoner. We will explore these five lessons – all mystical experiences – in what follows.

However, a few preliminary questions deserve a brief consideration. Might these five lessons have actually occurred in a different order? Is the sequence in which Ignatius records them trustworthy? Does this sequence have some significance other than the chronological? Thirty or so years had passed since his stay in Manresa. Memory, especially at that remove, can be weak or capricious. So, yes – the experiences could have occurred in a different order and Ignatius could have been confused. However, even granting this possibility, it is difficult not to see what happened on the banks of the Cardoner as the climax – the last in the series of lessons. It has all the marks of an integrative or synthesising experience (see Chapter 4).

However, leaving aside the possibility of memory loss, another question is worth considering. Has Ignatius chosen to structure his narrative theologically rather than chronologically? This would mean that he is not simply giving a description of his visions in the order in which he remembers them occurring, but – at least implicitly – he is proposing an interpretation of them. Accurate chronology is not his priority. We might ask, for instance, if this is the reason that he begins with his vision of the Trinity? Even if it did not come first in the actual sequence, Ignatius wants to affirm that the Trinity is the *fons et origo* (source and origin) of everything else. Theologically it *has* to come first. All that follows – whether chronologically or not – is then understood as flowing from this inaugural vision.

Trinity

Ignatius begins his account of the first vision by stating: 'He was greatly devoted to the Most Holy Trinity, and every day he prayed to each of the three Persons.' The vision, therefore, was not the beginning of his devotion to the Trinity but its intensification – and even its validation.

> One day, as he was saying the Hours of Our Lady on the monastery's steps, his understanding was raised on high, so as to see the Most Holy Trinity under the aspect of three keys on a musical instrument, and as a result he shed many tears and sobbed so strongly that he could not control himself. Joining in a procession that came out of the monastery, that morning he could not hold back his tears until dinnertime, and after he had eaten he could not refrain from talking, with much joy and consolation, about the Most Holy Trinity, making use of different comparisons. (28)

The image of the three keys *(teclas)* of a musical instrument, which Ignatius uses to elucidate the mystery of the Trinity, is what catches most readers' attention. Although theologians have suggested many other images over the centuries, the musical keys producing a single harmonious sound is as good a way as any of imaging the divine Three in One. It is inadequate, of course, as Ignatius well knew. The Trinitarian mystery is inexpressible.

However, there is much more of interest in this short passage than simply the central image. Consider the force of Ignatius's reaction to the revelation he had received: 'He shed many tears and sobbed so strongly that he could not control himself.' 'He could not hold back his tears until dinnertime.' Tears, as we know from other writings of Ignatius, came easily to him. He regarded them as a gift from God – a grace.[24] He trusted their authenticity

---

24 A number of times in the *Spiritual Exercises* Ignatius urges the retreatant to ask God for tears, e.g. (55). He also includes tears in his definition of consolation: 'Similarly, this consolation is experienced when the soul sheds tears which move it to love for its

because they were totally spontaneous and could not be fabri-cated. Thoughts might need to be sifted and scrutinised – as did feelings – but tears conveyed an unambiguous meaning. On this occasion they took the form not just of quiet weeping, but of rack-ing sobs. He had no control over them. They were witnessing to the depth of the encounter between Ignatius and the Trinity – the awesome coming together of the human and the divine.

Consider also how, after his evening meal when the tears had run their course, Ignatius felt an overwhelming urge to speak to other people about the Trinity. Towards the end of Chapter 1 we saw how Julian of Norwich was convinced that her 'showings' were not meant to benefit herself alone but had to be shared with others. Something similar is happening to Ignatius here, so that 'he could not refrain from talking, with much joy and consolation, about the Most Holy Trinity, making use of different compari-sons'. Note that he called on a number of comparisons – not only that of the three musical keys. Where did these other images or comparisons come from? Had they also been part of his vision? Or were they coming to him spontaneously as he spoke? We have no way of knowing.

This interaction with others did not diminish his ongoing per-sonal delight in the Trinity. He was experiencing 'much joy and consolation' in speaking, just as he had felt on the monastery's steps that morning. Sharing was not leading to any loss of what he had received – a fear experienced by some. At Loyola too, he had shared with his elder brother and members of the household the fruits of his reading and prayer (11). Now he does the same in Manresa with anyone willing to listen.

In terms of broader consequences, Ignatius is hearing a call, mediated by his mystical experience, *aiudar a las almas* (to help others). The principal way of doing this is going to be spiritual conversation – of which this sharing of his vision of the Trinity

Lord – whether they are tears of grief for its own sins, or about the Passion of Christ our Lord, or about other matters directly ordered to his service and praise' (316).

is an early example. Soon it will include the giving of the Spiritual Exercises – a ministry with spiritual conversation at its core. Later still, spiritual conversation will permeate the Jesuit Constitutions – both as a proposed way of living together, and as the 'engine' of all Jesuit ministries.

This vision of the Trinity was known to the close friends of Ignatius. In the earliest biographies, composed by Laínez and Polanco, we find an intriguing detail that is not mentioned in the *Autobiography*. Polanco, dealing with Ignatius's sojourn at Manresa, writes:

> He gained during this period so much illumination from God Our Lord that he was enlightened and consoled in almost all the mysteries of faith; and this was especially so with regard to the sublime mystery of the Most Holy Trinity. In this he came to know so much and with such delight in his spirit that, although he was a simple layman, who had no education except for being able to read and write in Spanish, he began to write a book about the Trinity.[25]

Unfortunately, this book has not survived. Later in the century Pedro de Ribadeneira[26] claimed that it consisted of over eighty pages. This may imply that the book was still in the possession of Ignatius during his early years in Rome and that he had shown it to the young Ribadeneira. Ignatius himself does not refer to it in any of his known writings. He may have either lost it (less likely) or destroyed it before his death (more likely).

---

25 Diego Laínez and Juan Polanco, *The First Biographies of St Ignatius Loyola*. Translated and edited by Joseph A. Munitiz SJ. Oxford: Way Books, 2019, 48. Henceforth referred to as *First Biographies*.

26 Pedro de Ribadeneira (1526–1611) was born in Toledo. He was received into the Society in Rome at fourteen years of age, days before the order was officially confirmed by Pope Paul III. He was later to write the official biography of Ignatius at the behest of St Francis Borgia. In English: *Pedro de Ribadeneira, The Life of Ignatius of Loyola*, translated by Claude Pavur SJ. St Louis, MO: Institute of Jesuit Sources, 2014.

The passage that we have been examining in the *Autobiography* ends with the words: 'This experience remained with him for the rest of his life, so that whenever he prayed to the Most Holy Trinity he felt great devotion.' This compelling statement underlines the continuity between Ignatius's orientation towards the Trinity in Manresa (1522) and his later (mid-1540s in Rome) almost total immersion in the Trinity – as recorded in his *Spiritual Diary*. This will be the subject of Chapter 6.

Creation

The second lesson is presented more briefly. Ignatius is clearly having difficulty in communicating its details and in explaining its meaning.

> One day it was granted him to understand, with great spiritual joy, the way in which God had created the world. He seemed to see a white object with rays stemming from it, from which God made light. He neither knew how to explain these things nor did he fully remember the spiritual lights that God had then imprinted on his soul. (29)

Ignatius's honesty may be admirable, but it does not help us to make sense of this vision. A white object from which rays are emanating is a rather opaque image. Yet he is unable to remember or explain anything further. *How* Ignatius understood God creating the world remains unknown to us. The most striking part of his narrative is not the image itself but the great spiritual joy that accompanied it. He remembers this joy even though he had forgotten most of what had brought it about! He remembers the joy because of its intensity, but also perhaps because it had guaranteed for him the authenticity of the vision.

Most visions – maybe all visions – are influenced by the prior experience of the visionary. They emanate from within the visionary's unique sensibility – and their religious and cultural worldview. God chooses to speak in the 'language' of the person to whom the revelation is given. As a child, Ignatius would have been taught the doctrine of *creatio ex nihilo* (creation out of nothing) – even if not yet the theological terminology. He would have believed, indeed taken for granted, that God created the world personally and by a direct intervention. The vision at Manresa must have worked within these parameters. It did not anticipate later scientific research on the origins of the universe – such as the Big Bang Theory – or later theological developments that sought to take such hypotheses into account.

Eucharist

While the lesson on the Trinity occurred on the steps of the Dominican church, this third lesson – on the Eucharist – was given inside this church during Mass. It is evident that Ignatius felt strongly drawn to attend Mass, and he did so regularly during his stay in Manresa. However, this is the first occasion when he records something extraordinary happening to him during a Mass. It was not to be his last such experience. Especially in his later years, then a priest and living in Rome, mystical experiences during Mass had become the norm rather than the exception. We will return to this phenomenon when exploring the *Spiritual Diary* in Chapter 6. This third lesson in Manresa, therefore, apart from its intrinsic value, also points forward to what was to come.

> One day, while in town and attending Mass in the church attached to the above-mentioned monastery [of the Dominicans], he saw with inward eyes, at the time of the elevation of the body of the Lord, some white rays coming from above. But after so long a time he is now unable to adequately explain this; nevertheless, he clearly saw with his understanding how our Lord Jesus Christ was present in this most holy Sacrament. (29)

Like his account of the second lesson on creation, this passage provides little by way of explanation. We are given an image of white rays coming from above at the elevation of the host. These rays are seen by Ignatius's inward eyes only. This emphasis may lead us to think once more of the spiritual senses (see Chapter 1). Many of Ignatius's visions were of this interior kind (see the fourth lesson below). However, there is no indication of how this vision helped his understanding of Christ's presence in the host. Once again we have to accept his apology for not being able to explain the lesson better due to the length of time that has elapsed.

Nevertheless, we could speculate about the upward and downward movements that Ignatius describes. The white rays descend *from above* at the precise moment when the priest lifts up the host *from below*. The rays, presumably coming from heaven and representing Christ, enter the host raised above the earth – transforming what is material (from below) into what is spiritual (from above) – the risen Christ's very self. Simultaneously, Christ now offers himself totally (upward movement) to his Father at the hands of the priest – although the raising of the host is, strictly speaking, not so much an offering to God as a showing to the faithful who are present. Such speculation may well go beyond what Ignatius wrote or intended to say. It sits somewhat uncomfortably with our contemporary liturgical sensibilities. Nevertheless, it is thought-provoking, and is likely compatible with the Catholic theology and Eucharistic devotion of the sixteenth century.

Humanity of Christ; Our Lady

More easily understood, at least to some degree, are the two visions that Ignatius brings together as the fourth lesson. A significant departure from the first three lessons is that the visions of Christ were not once-off occurrences. They repeated themselves many times and Ignatius underlines their frequency. They happened not only in Manresa but during his travels over the following years.[27]

---

27 Ignatius does not state *unambiguously* that he had a vision of Our Lady in Manresa, simply that he has seen her in a form similar to that of Christ. This could have happened subsequent to his departure from the town.

During prayer he often, and for an extended period of time, saw with inward eyes the humanity of Christ, whose form appeared to him as a white body, neither very large not very small; nor did he see any differentiation of members. He often saw this in Manresa; and if he was to say twenty times or forty times, he would not presume to say that he was lying. He saw it again when he was in Jerusalem, and once more when he was on his way to Padua. He has also seen Our Lady in similar form, without differentiation of members. (29)

It is somewhat curious that Ignatius describes this vision as being of the humanity of Christ – not simply as a vision of Christ. What he sees – with inward eyes, as in the third lesson – is a white body, or something like a white body, without any differentiation of members. In other words, Christ has no distinguishable torso, head, arms or legs – nothing that we might regard as necessary signs of a person's humanity. Yet Ignatius asserts that it is the *humanity* of Christ that he sees. Why is it important for him to stress this? And how does he recognise this humanity? Is he given an intuition that allows him to see beyond the image of the white body?[28]

The frequency of these visions in and after Manresa points to the centrality of Christ in his evolving spirituality. We might even dare to call most of these visions 'ordinary' – not in a reductive sense – but as in the liturgical term 'ordinary time'. They were mystical experiences that, especially after Manresa, had their context – not in dramatic turning points in his life – but in his daily prayer and his deeply felt devotion. Furthermore, the emphasis on the humanity of Christ is reflected in the *Spiritual Exercises* which, in their essentials, grew out of Ignatius's experiences in Manresa. We recall the grace of the Second Week, which

---

28 None of these issues arises in relation to his vision of Mary and the Child Jesus in Loyola. That was a simpler form of vision – possibly seen with his bodily eyes, or conjured up by his feverish imagination.

is described as 'an interior knowledge of our Lord, who became human for me, that I may love him more intensely and follow him more closely' (104).

It is noteworthy how Ignatius refers to a white object of some kind, and/or to (white) rays, in three of these four visions: 'a white object with rays stemming from it' (creation); 'some white rays coming from above' (Eucharist); 'as a white body – no differentiation of members' (humanity of Christ). Some writers think that such 'white' images *always* connote Christ. Such an interpretation would place Christ at the heart of creation as well as (more obviously) in the sacrament of the Eucharist, and in his self-identification with us in his humanity. Everything, it is argued, flows from the primordial experience – Ignatius's vision of the Trinity – the matrix of all reality. This is certainly a rich vein of theological reflection and worth pursuing.

The apostolic dimension
Before introducing the third lesson (Eucharist), Ignatius tells of a decision that he made around this time. In spite of its location in the text, this decision has no specific link with any one of the five lessons. It emerges out of all that is happening while he is being 'taught by God' – both within himself and in his contact with other people.

> It was likewise in Manresa – where he stayed for almost a year, and after experiencing divine consolations, and seeing the fruit that he was bringing forth in the souls he was helping – that he abandoned those extremes he had previously practised and began to cut his nails and hair. (29)

Ignatius, as we have seen, was always keen to engage in spiritual conversation with anyone who was willing – speaking about God and his own experiences in prayer. He noticed how an increasing number of people appreciated this interaction and how he was bringing forth fruit in their souls. This convinced him that God wanted him to continue this practice and to look on it as a spiritual ministry entrusted to him. For this to happen more easily and with a wider range of people, he needed to become more approachable. The extreme penances that he had been undertaking, and his practice of letting his nails and hair grow uncontrollably long, would need to be abandoned. They had sometimes made people hesitant to approach him – or fearful of being approached by him – as he had seemed either odd or threatening, if not both. So he came to understand that he needed to become more ordinary in his appearance, manner and dress – an insight that was to reappear later, in a broader context, in the Jesuit Constitutions.[29]

Although to most people this conclusion might have been obvious, it was not so to Ignatius. He was so caught up in – even obsessed by – his extreme austerities that he only came to understand the need for moderation in the light of his mystical experiences. He learned that he had to let go of something good – his penitential lifestyle – for the sake of something better – more fruitful interaction with others.[30] A spirituality that had been overly focused on himself needed to morph into one that prioritised the needs of others. It had taken God's mystical gifts to convince him of this truth.

An audacious claim

At the end of describing the fourth lesson (humanity of Christ), Ignatius makes an audacious claim. Referring to *all* his experiences of being taught by God he writes:

> These things that he saw at that time fortified him and gave him such great support to his faith that many times

---

29 'What pertains to food, sleep, and the use of the other things necessary or proper for living, will be ordinary.' *Constitutions* (580).

30 Ignatius is using two criteria that will later appear in the Principle and Foundation of the *Spiritual Exercises* (23). The first is known as *tantum quantum*: 'We ought to use these things to the extent that they help us toward our end, and free ourselves from them to the extent that they hinder us from it.' The second is known as the *magis* (more or greater): 'We ought to desire and choose only that which is more conducive to the end for which we are created.'

he thought to himself: if there were no Scriptures to teach us these matters of faith, he would still resolve to die for them on the basis of what he had seen. (29)

This passage will need to be kept in mind when, in Chapter 7, we reflect on how Ignatius fell under suspicion of *alumbradismo*. This term was given to a movement, mostly confined to Spain, of people who were accused of claiming direct enlightenment from the Holy Spirit. As a result, and in varying degrees, they were thought to hold that they did not need the Church to guide them. Such a suspicion tainted the reputation of many Catholics who were orthodox in their beliefs but who, like Ignatius, experienced mystical gifts. A discussion of these issues can make a valuable contribution to our understanding of the mysticism of Ignatius. Should it be considered orthodox or heterodox? For now, it is sufficient to become alert to some of the issues involved.

Chapter 4

Beside the Cardoner:
The Exceptional Enlightenment

Ignatius's description of the first four lessons that he received in Manresa is brief and concise. Along with the forgetfulness to which he confesses, his words also give an impression of hiding much more than they reveal. With the notable exception of the revelation of the Trinity, his account *points to* his feelings of elation and consolation rather than communicating them in a way that might warm the reader's heart. This trait of instinctive or deliberate reticence is likely to have been, in great part, the outcome of his fear of vainglory. It has also been attributed to his lacking a capacity to communicate imaginatively – as, for example, his near contemporary Teresa of Ávila (1515–1582) did so fluently and with such immediacy.

Nonetheless, Ignatius did *not* lack imagination or a willingness to use it. He had written poetry in his days as a courtier – an art that explores the world of imagination. As he convalesced in Loyola, he had entered imaginatively, and with a natural facility and eagerness, into the romances of chivalry and the lives of Christ and the saints. It was through his imagination that he explored possible future scenarios in his life – seeing himself as a swashbuckling knight or as a poor beggar following Christ. However, in the *Autobiography*, when he attempts to communicate imaginatively, he does so with sobriety rather than exuberance – drawing small monochrome sketches rather than painting large canvases covered with a riot of colour.

Centrality of understanding
There was much more than imagination at play in Ignatius's first four visions in Manresa. Indeed, the core experience in each was

intellectual rather than imaginative. They were, after all, 'lessons'. He was being taught by God – instructed in the central doctrines of Christian faith. This is not always underscored by commentators who are insensitive to, or who choose to overlook, the ecclesial dimension of his mysticism. The images that surfaced were at the service of his gaining insight into all that God had revealed – and of inserting him more deeply into the life of the Church.

Notice the phrases he uses in the *Autobiography*: 'his understanding was raised on high'; 'it was granted him to understand'; 'he clearly saw with his understanding'. This undeniable stress on the understanding does not rule out the possibility, even likelihood, of accompanying feelings – what in broad terms we call consolations. Indeed, Ignatius mentions them frequently. Nevertheless, neither the feelings nor the images constitute the substance of the experience – this lies in the understanding.

Nevertheless, as readers of the *Autobiography* we rely on the images that Ignatius presents to us. They constitute both a starting point and a prism. By evoking and exploring them, we aim to reach some appreciation of what Ignatius was given to understand. But for Ignatius, the movement seems to have been in the opposite direction. He was given understanding – the core of the mystical experience – and an image accompanied or followed it. Did understanding and image come simultaneously? Was it the image that mediated his understanding? Or was the image more of an aide-memoire for himself? Or a way of more easily communicating his experience to others? However we answer these difficult questions, one thing is sure: *Ignatius had the mystical understanding and we do not.* So it is we, not he, who depend more on the images.

An enlightenment of the spirit

When it comes to the fifth lesson[31] – on the banks of the River Cardoner – there is no vision for the outer or inner eyes to see.

---

31 Called *la eximia ilustración* by Nadal, this phrase has been repeated to this day. I have translated it in the title of this chapter as 'the exceptional enlightenment'.

Ignatius accentuates this – marking a clear distinction between the fifth and the earlier lessons. This absence of a vision or image leads to an even stronger focus on the understanding but deprives the reader of an entry point into that understanding.

> As he sat there the eyes of his understanding were opened and though he saw no vision he understood and perceived many things, numerous spiritual things as well as matters touching on faith and learning, and this was with an elucidation so bright that all these things seemed new to him. (30)

Here da Câmara inserts a comment in the margins of the text: 'This left his understanding so very enlightened that he felt he was another man with another mind.'

It can even be argued – and very plausibly – that Ignatius's primary purpose as he recounts what happened at Cardoner is not so much to convey *what* he had been taught as simply *that* he had been taught (by God). We recall his claim that 'During this period God was dealing with him in the same way a schoolteacher deals with a child while instructing him' (27). Ignatius wants readers – primarily his fellow Jesuits for whom the narrative was intended (see Chapter 2) – to be convinced of this. He had been asked to tell *how* God had led him, but he must first show *that* God had led him. These two aims are interconnected but the latter enjoys a certain logical priority.

Furthermore, by emphasising this claim for the divine origin of what he had received, Ignatius is offering the reader a justification or an *apologia* for the subsequent choices affecting his life. Many of these were in line with tradition – received wisdom within the Church – but others were more idiosyncratic or innovative, and raised the suspicions of the Inquisition. Presenting an *apologia* before tribunals became a regular, if unwelcome, necessity. He needed to defend his orthodoxy – not just for his personal vindication, but to maintain his credibility as a Christian teacher. Apostolic outreach had become of central concern to him.

We might say that Ignatius acts like an Old Testament prophet who has no licence from the Temple priesthood or the religious authorities to teach or preach. Instead, the prophet lays claim to a higher authorisation – one received directly from God at the time of the prophet's call. In Chapter 7 we will examine some of the criticism that Ignatius encountered, and the grounds for this criticism. We will see that, as with the prophets, much of this opposition flowed from his claim to be directly enlightened by God.

Ignatius's description of Cardoner continues:

> He cannot expound in detail what he then understood, for they were many things, but he can state that he received such a lucidity in understanding that during the course of his entire life – now having passed his sixty-second year – if he were to gather all the helps he received from God and everything he knew, and add them together, he does not think they would add up to all that he received on that one occasion. (30)

This astonishing statement needs to be interpreted with some care. It does not necessarily mean that Cardoner was the acme or summit of Ignatius's mystical experiences, however foundational and life-changing it was. It happened at a particular, and relatively early, stage in his spiritual journey, during that extended period we know as his conversion. Cardoner played a unique, perhaps irreplaceable, role at this stage in his development – something he never hid from his companions. Much later, when one or other of them made a reference in their writings to Manresa, they often meant Cardoner, or vice versa. It was as if they understood that Cardoner encapsulated all the graces that Ignatius received during those eleven pivotal months.

However, even granting the lasting impression that Cardoner made on Ignatius, and despite what he says in the *Autobiography*, it can be argued that some of his later mystical experiences were more profound *in terms of union with God*. This is possibly true of the vision at La Storta, and certainly true of those in Rome. These later experiences will be discussed in Chapters 5 and 6.

What then are we to make of Ignatius's claim? It can plausibly be interpreted as meaning that Cardoner was unsurpassed for him *in a didactic sense* – as an experience of being taught by God. It brought him 'a lucidity of understanding'. It was the most profound and influential of God's lessons – excelling the totality of the four other Manresa experiences, and any later mystical experience of a similar (didactic) kind. The understanding and wisdom that Ignatius was granted on the banks of the Cardoner continued to enlighten and inspire him. He was to put them at God's service along the road ahead, up to and including the foundation of the Society of Jesus.

During his years as Superior General Ignatius referred to Cardoner frequently, especially during the composition of the Constitutions. When questioned about some decision he had made about Jesuit lifestyle or practice, he would refer to 'something that happened to me at Manresa' (meaning the Cardoner). This enigmatic phrase led some of the early Jesuits to strange exaggerations as to what Ignatius actually learned at the Cardoner. Some imagined him seeing there – in every detail – the future form of the Society of Jesus. Among the proponents of this theory was da Câmara, who wrote in his *Memoriale*:

> This experience [Cardoner] was a great illumination of the understanding in which Our Lord at Manresa showed to our Father these and many other things later established in the Society.[32]

Myth and reality
Such an embellished myth could only have been created or believed by individuals with an excess of reverence for their

32 *Remembering Iñigo*, 84. See ch. 2, fn. 7.

charismatic leader. The pattern is not unfamiliar from the lives of other personalities in history, for whose followers their leader embodies preternatural knowledge, foresight and wisdom. This transference – for such it is in psychological language – becomes the raw material for the emergence of myths. However, these tell us more about the subconscious aspirations of the followers than about the leader who is being idolised.

At this point we need to consider a passage from Nadal. His words are frequently quoted and gain extra currency from the closeness of his collaboration with Ignatius over many years in Rome – the period when Ignatius was working on the Constitutions. It was to Nadal that Ignatius entrusted the promulgation and interpretation of the final – although not yet officially approved – version of the Constitutions in Jesuit communities in Spain and Portugal. He saw Nadal as the person who best understood his own mind. Nadal writes:

> Ignatius always prized this gift [Cardoner] highly; because of it he conceived a profound modesty and humility; from it there began to shine on his countenance an indescribable spiritual light and alacrity. He was wont to refer to that one grace and light whenever he was questioned either about serious matters or about some reasons for the way of life in the Society – as though he had seen on that one occasion the inner causes and bases of all things.[33]

Nadal was not totally innocent in the emergence of the myth referred to above. He was a fervent admirer of Ignatius and prone to great enthusiasms. For example, he held that God would lead the Society of Jesus – and individual Jesuits – in the same way

---

33   From *Dialogi*, a work written in 1562–65, defending the Institute or way of life of the Society of Jesus.

as God had led Ignatius. This would be their path to holiness and would guarantee the fruitfulness of their ministries. He hammered home this conviction at every opportunity. This was what lay behind his insistence that Ignatius tell his story (see Chapter 2).

Yet, in spite of his adulation of Ignatius, Nadal could not possibly have believed that the myth that was gaining traction among certain Jesuits was literally true. As one of those most conversant with Ignatius's methodology, and his protracted struggles in composing the Constitutions, Nadal knew that Ignatius did not simply write or dictate what he had already learned at the Cardoner. He had to bring all the key issues to prayer, consider them from all angles, and rely on the invaluable research being conducted by his multi-talented secretary, Polanco. In some respects, Polanco could be described as a co-author of the Constitutions. What is more, from time to time Ignatius even consulted Nadal himself. Nadal knew well that Cardoner did not provide Ignatius with any convenient shortcut.

A more balanced and subtle reading of what happened at Cardoner is called for. One of the more convincing interpretations is that Ignatius acquired in that momentous experience the gift of *discernment*. Cardoner, of course, had not been his first lesson in discernment. Before that – as he read and ruminated on the *Vita Christi* and *Flos Sanctorum* in Loyola – he had learned to become self-aware and to wonder. This led him to his first tentative steps in understanding his inner world – so full of mystery and paradox. However, after Cardoner, he understood that inner world better – and God's relationship with it. This led to an assurance in his subsequent decision-making that had previously been lacking. Cardoner was his ultimate, definitive enlightenment on the matter. It gave him a firm grasp of the theological basis of discernment, along with a highly sensitised skill in applying its principles. For this reason, it became the methodology he was to use in all his later decision-making.

This interpretation is widely accepted today – but it is not an entirely new interpretation. It can be found, at least in embryonic form, in Polanco's early biography of Ignatius.

> At the end of four months after his conversion – during which time, by making good use of the little light given him by the Lord, he made himself ready for His higher gifts – once when he was near a river, suddenly and quite unusually, he was granted by His divine mercy an admirable illumination of divine things, feeling an admirable delight in them, along with a great power of discretion of spirits, the good and the bad. As a result, he began to see everything with different eyes from before.[34]

New knowledge?

A recurring question in the interpretation of Cardoner is whether or not, along with the gift of discernment, Ignatius received *new knowledge* as part of his experience. Was the 'content' of his knowledge of God, and of God's plan for the world, increased or expanded? Some commentators answer in the affirmative – while steering clear of the myth discussed above. Appeal is made to Ignatius's words in the text of the *Autobiography*. However, while the text does not exclude such a reading, neither does it demand it. Let us recall the exact wording:

> He understood and perceived many things, numerous spiritual things as well as matters touching on faith and learning, and this was with an elucidation so bright that all these things seemed new to him. (30)

These words can legitimately mean that Ignatius was given an enhanced intellectual grasp of realities – secular as well as religious – that he already knew at some level. This is the more

---

34 *First Biographies*, 46.

probable meaning. If he had been receiving *new knowledge*, there would be no sense in his saying that 'all these things *seemed* new to him' – they would *in fact* have been new to him. However, he was seeing realities, with which he was to some extent familiar, in a more penetrating light and with a greater profundity. Such a reading also fits well with Polanco's statement above: 'He began to see everything with different eyes from before.' The change lay in his enhanced ability to see, not in the range of things seen.

Furthermore, since Ignatius speaks of Cardoner immediately after his description of the first four lessons – presuming that it is the climax of an interconnected series – it is likely that he is referring inter alia to a deeper understanding of the Trinity, creation, Eucharist, the humanity of Christ, and Our Lady. These were certainly not new objects of knowledge, or newly discovered religious truths. But even they – which he had already been privileged to see 'mystically' – *seemed* as new in the vivid intuitive grasp with which he was gifted at the Cardoner.

Interconnectedness

Either interpretation of Cardoner – that there was *some* or *much* new content in Ignatius's experience there, or that there was *no* new content but rather a radical change in how he saw reality – allows for the next proposition. This holds that a vital part of his enlightenment was a grasp of the *interconnectedness* of the truths, new or old, whose meaning he saw. There was a bringing together in his consciousness of matters of the spirit, of faith, and of secular learning. This was not the conclusion of a logical progression in his thinking so much as a piercing intuition. Such interconnectedness may well be – it certainly comes close to – what Nadal meant when he wrote of Ignatius's seeing 'the inner causes and bases of all things'. It may also have constituted a crucial part of what he was being taught about discernment. In turn, this points to an additional explanation of how the Cardoner experience could become the touchstone in his future decision-making.

The difficulties that we encounter in the making of a decision often arise from lacking knowledge or mindfulness of interconnections and interrelations. Firstly, we may not sufficiently recognise interconnections among the natural and human realities with which we are dealing – persons, situations, issues, needs and so forth. Secondly, we can be blind to the interconnections that exist between these natural and human realities on the one hand, and, on the other, the divine realities that transcend them, yet mysteriously impinge on them. A conscious awareness of all these interconnections – horizontal and vertical – would facilitate our discernment and decision-making enormously. Such an awareness was almost certainly the greatest gift bestowed on Ignatius at the Cardoner.

Learning – sacred and secular

This grasp of the interconnectedness of all realities – human and divine – also shows itself in Ignatius's attitude towards learning. It is extraordinary, if not unique, to find secular learning or scholarship *(letras)* being a component of a mystical enlightenment – as happened to Ignatius at Cardoner. He specifies it quite unmistakably. What this aspect of his illumination involved, or even could have involved, is impossible to imagine – especially if we hold that there was no new content in his experience (see discussion above). However, we do know that in subsequent years he displayed immense respect for learning. This combined an appreciation of scholarship as a value in itself, allied with a conviction that learning could play a key role in furthering his desire to be of help to others.

After he returned to Spain from a pilgrimage to the Holy Land in 1524, he took to studying Latin grammar alongside young boys in Barcelona. He then proceeded to Alcalá and Salamanca, studying somewhat haphazardly in their universities. Finally, he made his way to Paris where he arrived in 1528. Here he gave himself to the serious study of philosophy and theology. His formal education culminated when he graduated from the University of Paris with a Master of Arts degree in 1535. It is easy to forget that Ignatius – best known to us as a mystic, spiritual director and founder of a religious order – chose to spend eleven years of his adult life in formal education.

As to secular learning specifically, Ignatius neither demonised nor canonised it. He was no Savonarola, railing against the study of pagan classics and instigating the Bonfire of the Vanities.[35] On the other hand, he certainly did not think of secular learning as superior to, still less capable of replacing revealed truth – as proclaimed by the Church and explored by the theologians. However, he recognised that sacred and secular knowledge were complementary dimensions of the *one* Truth. Both had their origins in God. Hence, both must be fostered by the individual Christian and within the human community.

Some people today refer to Ignatius as a Christian humanist – presumably in the same mould as other Renaissance thinkers such as Thomas More (1478–1535) and Desiderius Erasmus (1469–1536). This is something of an exaggeration. Ignatius remained steeped in medieval culture – especially in religious matters – even while embracing many Renaissance values. This intriguing combination sets him apart from More and Erasmus, who were more fully representative of the 'new learning' of the Renaissance. Nevertheless, comparisons between the three men are enlightening when they are considered together as part of a broadly based and irenic Catholic reformation. We can at least say that Ignatius shared the two scholars' appreciation of, and commitment to learning – even if he never attained, or aspired to, their extraordinary erudition.

Jesuit Constitutions

An awareness of the interconnectedness of the human and the divine underpins the praxis of the Society of Jesus. Ignatius wrote

---

35 Girolamo Savonarola (1452–1498), an Italian Dominican friar who preached against the corruption and licentiousness of Renaissance Florence. He was condemned as a heretic and executed.

into its Constitutions an insistence that young Jesuits should become proficient in secular *and* ecclesiastical studies. This wide-ranging and inclusive formation programme was aimed at preparing them for a broad range of possible ministries, and at enabling them to adapt to different cultures when missioned abroad. The Society, after all, was to be an international order with a worldwide remit to evangelise. To achieve its aim, it needed a meticulously prepared and – from a religious life perspective – a ground-breaking set of guidelines on studies.

Subsequently, this same grasp of the interconnectedness of all things was seen as justifying the entry of the Society into the apostolate of education. In 1549 Ignatius agreed that Jesuits could take responsibility for schools and colleges for boys who were *not* preparing to enter the Society – or in today's terminology, lay students. Up until then Jesuits only taught aspirants to enter the Society, and younger Jesuits in formation. This new and wider educational ministry had not been part of the original plan and was not mentioned in earlier documents. It was in clear discontinuity with the ideals of mobility and availability that had been among the primary characteristics of the Society. Ignatius was prophetically alert to the apostolic potential of the ministry, although curiously blind to many of its consequences.

Colleges began to tie down an increasingly large number of Jesuits over the following four centuries, and the Society lost much of its freedom of movement and ability to respond quickly to new situations. Thousands of Jesuits who volunteered to go to mission countries were refused permission as they were needed as teachers at home. It was only after the Second Vatican Council that this development was critiqued and addressed, restoring much of the original mobility and availability that marked the Society at its foundation.

Afterthoughts
When we reflect on all five lessons that God gave Ignatius at Manresa (see Chapters 3 and 4), the evidence overwhelmingly

points to what happened at Cardoner as having the most powerful and lasting influence. Ignatius himself tells us so in the *Autobiography*, and this verdict is corroborated by close associates such as Laínez, Polanco and Nadal. This does not mean that Cardoner can be considered in isolation, as though it had no significant link with anything that happened earlier. On the contrary, it is better to see Cardoner as emerging from all that had preceded it – even as a gathering together of the fruits of the first four lessons. These fruits are then drawn deep down into Ignatius's soul until they coalesce. There they become one comprehensive lesson, one piercing enlightenment. It is as though Pentecost has happened for Ignatius and, like the apostles in *Acts*, he emerges a new man, on fire with zeal.

The difficulties we experience in interpreting Cardoner should not surprise us. After all, who can fully understand Pentecost? Any attempted exegesis can only be partial, even tentative. These obscurities were openly acknowledged among the early companions. Polanco wrote: 'Father Ignatius explained to no one the secret of this vision, since it was so hard to communicate his experiences. But he did mention the fact to them.'[36] So we know that something highly significant happened at the Cardoner ('fact'), but Ignatius was unable to communicate its essence ('secret'). Part of this inability is due to the absence of any imagery. We recall that, *pace* Polanco's use of the word, Ignatius tells us that 'he saw no vision'. He had not received, nor been able to create, an image to latch on to and use in recounting what happened. All this means that, in large part, we have to work backwards – which we have been doing – tracing a line from what we know of the effects of Cardoner on Ignatius to the original mystical experience. That is the only methodology that carries any hope of our gaining insight. What actually happened on that river bank? We can never entirely be sure – but it was seismic!

---

36 From a life of Ignatius written in 1574.

CHAPTER 5

Vision of La Storta:
Placed with the Son

Earlier we remarked on the importance of context in attempting to understand any of Ignatius's mystical experiences. His eleven-month stay in Manresa was a key part of his conversion – a time for strengthening and deepening the roots that had first been planted during his convalescence in Loyola. It was a period during which he saw himself as being taught by God. His mystical experiences there were a key part of that teaching. They had primarily a didactic purpose – even though they also had other features and effects. In retrospect, Ignatius saw them as preparing him for all the developments that lay ahead in his life – all that God would ask of him. They became part of who he was, and gave him a resource on which he could draw – especially in times of crisis and decision-making.

The context for the vision at La Storta was quite different. Fifteen years had passed and Ignatius was no longer a lone individual with little education seeking to find himself and God. He was a Master of Arts from the prestigious University of Paris. While there, he had gathered together a group of his fellow students with whom he shared his evangelical ideals and plans. A central desire of these 'first companions' – as they came to be called – was to embark on a communal pilgrimage to the Holy Land. (This would have been a second such pilgrimage for Ignatius, though on the previous journey in 1523 he had travelled alone). Their intention was not just the traditional one of seeking devotion by retracing the steps of Christ, but to minister to the Christians and Muslims living in the region.

When war broke out between Venice and the Turks, the Mediterranean became a no-go area and all pilgrimages were forbidden for reasons of safety. The companions decided to go to Rome instead and put themselves at the service of the Pope. First they received priestly ordination in Venice in 1537, after which they spent three months leading a semi-eremitical lifestyle in the area around Vicenza. During this time, they combined periods of withdrawal into solitude with engagement in pastoral work.

Return of consolations

Much was happening for all the companions throughout their stay in northern Italy. In retrospect they saw it as a time of preparation for the founding of the Society of Jesus in 1540. However, for Ignatius there also occurred a change in his inner life that he chose to record in the *Autobiography*.

> During the period that he was in Vicenza, he received many spiritual visions and many rather ordinary consolations (it was just the opposite when he was in Paris), but especially when he began to prepare for his ordination in Venice and when he was getting ready to celebrate Mass. Also during his journeys, he enjoyed great supernatural visitations of the kind that he used to have when he was in Manresa. (95)

While we may regret an absence of specific detail in this passage, the core of what Ignatius describes is nonetheless of great interest. In Chapters 3 and 4 we examined his mystical experiences in Manresa. These or similar graces had been absent during his Parisian years, but had returned when he was residing in the Venice-Vicenza area (January 1536 to October 1537). He associates them especially with the period before and after his priestly ordination. We will notice references to priesthood appearing regularly from now on – they will be worth pondering.

Why had consolations been absent in Paris? One suggestion – plausible if not conclusive – is that serious, full-time study tends to induce aridity in a person's soul, draining it of affectivity. In the case of Ignatius, this tendency would have been exacerbated by the distinctly cerebral nature of scholastic learning – along with the punishing university schedule. There were long hours devoted to lectures that began early in the morning, and much stress on logic and dialectic. Students were expected to engage in endless discussions and the defence of a constant stream of theses. The mind, but not the heart, was being exercised and stretched – the rational faculty dominated the affective. This was not fertile soil for spiritual or mystical experiences.[37]

Along the Via Cassia

When the companions felt ready to present themselves to the Pope – in hope of expediting their discernment about their future – they set off for Rome. It was the end of October 1537. The *Autobiography* takes up the story:

> They went to Rome in three or four groups; the pilgrim was with Favre[38] and Laínez, and on this journey God often visited him in a special way. After he had been ordained a priest, he decided to wait another year before celebrating Mass, preparing himself for that event and praying to our Lady to place him with her Son. One day, a few miles before reaching Rome, while praying in a church, he felt a great change in his soul and so clearly did he see God the Father place him with Christ, His Son, that he had

---

37 There is no evidence that Ignatius underwent a Dark Night of the Soul, such as that described by St John of the Cross, during his studies in Paris.

38 Pierre Favre (1506–1546) hailed from the alpine region of Haute-Savoie. During his studies in Paris he shared a room with Ignatius and Francis Xavier. While still in Paris he became the first of the early companions to be ordained. Later, as a Jesuit, he travelled widely in Europe at Ignatius's behest.

no doubts that God the Father did place him with His Son. (96)[39]

The decision made by Ignatius to postpone celebrating mass for a year came from his lingering hope of still being able to reach the Holy Land within that time frame. It was there that he wanted to offer his first mass. By the following year, however, he had reluctantly accepted that this pilgrimage would not happen. On 25 December 1538 he celebrated his first mass in the chapel of the manger in the Roman basilica of Santa Maria Maggiore. This was the nearest he was going to get to Bethlehem – or anywhere else in the Holy Land – and the mass in that chosen location brought him great consolation.

The meaning of La Storta

The main key to interpreting the vision of La Storta is provided by Ignatius's words about 'praying to Our Lady to place him with her Son'. He had been making this petition regularly since he began preparing for his first Mass – therefore, while still in Northern Italy. Now it permeates his prayer as he journeys towards Rome along the Via Cassia in the company of Favre and Laínez.

The *Autobiography* draws our attention to his praying to Our Lady. However, this does not necessarily mean that he was not also praying – for the same grace – to Christ and the Father. The intended readership of his narrative – mostly his fellow Jesuits – would immediately have recognised the wording he uses as shorthand for the Triple Colloquy in the meditation on the Two Standards. Here the person making the Spiritual Exercises prays:

I beg [Our Lady] to obtain for me grace from her Son and Lord that I may be received under his standard; and first, in the most perfect spiritual poverty; and also, if his

---

39 This church, or wayside chapel, was located in the village of La Storta, just off the Via Cassia, approximately 17km from Rome. Hence Ignatius's vision is referred to simply as La Storta.

Divine Majesty should be served and if he should wish to choose me for it, to no less a degree of actual poverty; and second, in bearing reproaches and injuries, that through them I may imitate him more; if only I can do this without sin on anyone's part and without displeasure to the Divine Majesty. (147)

After this appeal to Our Lady, the retreatant then asks the same grace from the Son, 'that he may obtain it for me from the Father', and finally asks it from the Father, 'that he may grant it to me'.[40] This Triple Colloquy, as it is known, is pivotal to the dynamic of the Spiritual Exercises and is repeated frequently during the Second and Third Weeks. As he travels towards Rome, it expresses Ignatius's deepest desire at this critical point in his life.

He is not asking for a purely devotional experience – a comforting sense of being close to Christ. The fuller version of the prayer in the *Spiritual Exercises* – the Triple Colloquy – makes this abundantly clear. To be placed with Christ involves spiritual and even actual poverty, as well as the bearing of reproaches and insults. Ignatius wants not just to be placed *alongside* Christ – shoulder to shoulder, as it were – but to be drawn into his *experience* of life on earth. This has to include being one with Christ in his sufferings and in his dying. Ignatius has desired this grace since his time in Manresa. Now, however, conscious of his priesthood as a sharing in Christ's sacrificial priesthood, he needs to experience it at a deeper level.

Company of Jesus

But there was much more than his first mass on Ignatius's mind as he walked towards Rome. He was aware that a new stage in his life, and in that of his companions, was beginning, but he was as yet unsure of its contours. During their final weeks in northern

---

40 The phrases 'to be received under his standard' (*Spiritual Exercises*) and 'to be placed with her Son' (*Autobiography*) convey the same meaning for Ignatius.

Italy the companions had agreed that, if asked who they were, they would say that they were 'of the Company of Jesus' – in Italian, *Compagnía di Gesù*. Such enquiries were already being made of them – understandably so. The companions were priests: Why then were they not serving in parishes where the needs were so great? Was this not the purpose of their ordination? On the other hand, the companions were not religious: Why then were they sharing what looked like a life in common? What justified this practice? These were all valid questions.

In sixteenth-century Italy the word *'compagnía'* would have suggested some kind of confraternity or pious association – most likely one engaging in apostolic activity. Its best-known exemplar was the *Compagnía del Divino Amore* – Company of Divine Love – in Rome (founded in the late fifteenth century in Genoa). This included clergy as well as laity among its members. Ignatius and his companions saw in the word *'compagnía'* an easily identifiable, yet sufficiently imprecise term to use with interested enquirers. Their response had to be vague because they themselves did not yet know the full answers to the questions they were being asked.

Views vary as to how much significance can be read into the designation *at this point* of the *Compagnía* as being *'di Gesù'*. We know that the companions had reached consensus on the matter, although some sources attribute the initial proposal of the name to Ignatius. However, this decision was taken in order to meet a particular problem, in which context, adopting the title might be understood as a temporary or interim measure. The name had no legal status either civilly or ecclesiastically – just as the companions were still an informal group of priests who were simply 'friends in the Lord'.

Later in Rome, after the foundation of the new order, the situation was very different. The companions now had a corporate canonical status and a public presence in the Church. Yet in Paul III's bull of approbation, *Regimini militantis ecclesiae* (1540), there is an ambiguity – almost certainly deliberate – about the name. The text speaks of 'our Society, which we desire to be designated by the name of Jesus'.[41] This formulation allows for either 'Society of Jesus' or 'Society of the Holy Name of Jesus' – two forms that were used almost interchangeably during the following decade. Even some of the first companions – who had voted in Vicenza for calling themselves the 'Society of Jesus' – were among those who were using 'Society of the Holy Name of Jesus'. It would seem that so long as the name of Jesus appeared in the title, either version was acceptable. However, by 1550, 'Society of Jesus' was being universally employed, in large part on Ignatius's insistence.

Having the name of Jesus in the Society's title became a non-negotiable matter for Ignatius personally. It was a break with the tradition of calling religious orders after their founder (Benedictines, Franciscans) or after a place (Cistercians – founded in Cîteaux). But in spite of much external criticism he refused to change his mind. Many commentators hold that what happened at La Storta was crucial in bolstering his resolve. Polanco, having worked alongside Ignatius over many years, writes:

> In relation to this question of name, Father Master Ignatius received so many visitations from the one whose name they had adopted, and so many signs of his approval and confirmation of this title, that I heard Ignatius himself say he thought he would be going against God and would offend Him if he were to call in doubt how suitable and right this name was. Some people were saying that we were lifting ourselves up to the height of Jesus Christ and others were saying other things, but when, either by word of mouth or in writing, it was suggested that Ignatius change it, I remember him saying to me that even if all the members of the Society and everybody else were to be of the opinion that the name ought to be changed, provided

---

41 The word *'compañia'* is rendered in Latin as *'societas'* without any suggestion of a different meaning. In English *'societas'* becomes 'society.'

they were not such that they had to be obeyed under pain of sin, he alone would never agree.[42]

Liminality

The anthropological term *'liminality'* is frequently used in discussions of spirituality today. It refers to the experience of being in an in-between space or time. The term comes from the Latin word *'limen,'* meaning threshold. The best-known liminal deity is Janus, whose two faces look in opposite directions. He is the Roman god of the in-between. Being in a liminal space, leads to an awareness – frequently unsettling – that we are on the cusp of some new development in our lives. However, what this will be remains unknown – as do its consequences. We are made to live between a familiar past and an unfamiliar future.

This time of waiting, however difficult it may be, provides an opportunity for self-transformation and surrender. Embracing the uncertainty and the anxiety, we acquire a new sensibility to the world and to what lies beyond the world – to the mystery of life and to God. When we occupy this liminal space, the wall between the natural and the supernatural – between earth and heaven – becomes paper-thin. This is when personal breakthroughs are not only possible but are likely to occur. Even unusual psychic occurrences are not unexpected.

Throughout the journey to Rome, Ignatius was inhabiting two in-between spaces. The first was unique to himself; the second he shared with his companions – more immediately with the two who were accompanying him, Favre and Laínez. On a personal level he was in an in-between space – *after* his ordination and *before* his first mass (the date for which was still unknown). On a communal level, he and his companions occupied an in-between space – *after* their open-ended commitment (in Paris) to a ministerial lifestyle,[43] and *before* their discovery of the definitive form

42 *First Biographies*, 91.
43 Usually associated with the vows of Montmartre in 1534, which were renewed in the following years.

that this commitment was to take. This experience of liminality created the conditions for La Storta to happen – Ignatius becoming the direct recipient of the vision.

As an addendum, we might consider some brief words of Nadal. Here the writer gives us a striking description of what was happening in Ignatius at this time. Notice his use of the word 'road' as a metaphor, which draws our attention to the actual road that Ignatius travelled to Rome.

> Ignatius was following the Spirit; he was not running ahead of it. And yet he was being led gently, whither he did not know. He was not intending at that time to found the Order. Little by little, though, the road was opening up before him and he was moving along it, wisely ignorant *(quasi sapienter imprudens)*, with his heart placed very simply in Christ.[44]

To be 'wisely ignorant' is the opposite of being self-important or arrogant. It indicates a genuine humility – a virtue highly regarded in the Christian spiritual tradition. This is a grace frequently received when we are in a liminal space – enabling us to wait in faith and hope for our future to be revealed to us. This constitutes a high point of indifference – as Ignatius presents it in the *Spiritual Exercises* (23). It opens the door to many other graces – and even to mystical experience.

The vision itself

The terse description in the *Autobiography* of what transpired at La Storta omits almost all detail. It establishes that Ignatius understood the core of the vision as the Father placing him with the Son. This event he saw with his inner eye. Others added that he also heard the Father speak – presumably with his inner ear. In

---

44 From the *Dialogi* (1563).

any case, this was the response that Ignatius received to the prayer he had been making before and during this journey.

However, there were other aspects to the vision that Ignatius had either forgotten or was reluctant to talk about. In later years, whenever he was asked for more details, he would routinely reply, 'Ask Laínez. He knows what I told him.' This refers to the fact that, immediately after the vision, Ignatius spoke about it to his two travelling companions – Favre and Laínez. Since Favre was mostly away from Rome over the following years and died in 1547, Laínez became the obvious person for Ignatius to recommend as a reliable witness. Let us look at Laínez's fuller account.

He [Ignatius] told me that it seemed to him that God the Father had impressed on his heart the following words: 'I shall be favourable to you in Rome'. And not knowing what these words meant to indicate, our Father said: 'I do not know what will happen to us – perhaps we shall be crucified in Rome. He also said that it seemed to him he saw Christ carrying a cross on his shoulders and the Eternal Father nearby who said to Christ: 'I want you to take this man for your servant'. And so, Jesus actually received him and said: 'I want you to serve us'.[45]

Laínez's first addition

The Laínez version has two salient additions to what is contained in the *Autobiography*. These are worth exploring. The first is that, although Ignatius alone saw the vision, he intuitively understood it as revelatory for all his companions as well. Given that the purpose of their journey to Rome was to discern their common future, he interpreted the vision as advancing that discernment. It provided assurance that they – and not alone he – were on the right path.

45 From a talk given in Rome in 1559.

This corporate interpretation of the vision presages what Ignatius later refers to – especially in the Jesuit Constitutions – as 'the body of the Society'. When Jesus utters the words 'I want you to serve us', the pronoun 'you' is plural. Jesus wants this group of men, this body – with Ignatius during the vision acting as their representative – to serve 'us'. Jesus, too, is in a representative role – he is speaking on behalf of the Trinity. The human *Compagnía* (of the future Society of Jesus) is called on to serve the divine *Compagnía* (of the three Divine Persons). Of course, since the Society had not yet come into existence, this reading of the vision is, in part, retrospective.

It is noticeable that while the Father and the Son are explicitly present in the vision, the Holy Spirit is not. This is true of all the early accounts of La Storta and it corresponds with what we find in the *Spiritual Exercises*. The Spirit is not exactly absent, but his presence is hidden and needs to be inferred – as in the words of Jesus: 'I want you to serve us'. However, this apparent absence of the Spirit weakens, to some extent, the frequently made claim that La Storta is a Trinitarian vision. This claim, while not altogether untrue, needs nuance.

Laínez's second addition

The second addition provided by Laínez is that Ignatius finds himself placed – not with Christ in his public life – but with Christ carrying his cross. In the terminology of the *Spiritual Exercises*, he finds himself in the Third Week accompanying the suffering Christ on his journey to Calvary. He had been making a Second Week prayer – the Triple Colloquy of the Two Standards – but receives a Third Week grace.[46] Impulsively he interprets this as a warning that he and his companions may undergo crucifixion in Rome. He later modifies this to an expectation of persecutions – a

---

46 Second Week grace: An interior knowledge of Our Lord, who became human for me, that I may love him more intensely and follow him more closely (104). Third Week grace: Sorrow with Christ in sorrow; a broken spirit with Christ so broken; tears; and interior suffering because of the great suffering which Christ endured for me (203).

fate that did await them the following year (1538). Yet this explanation, even if defensible, fails to recognise the deeper meaning of the vision.

A far more important dynamic – and promise – is at play here. While the distinction between Second and Third Week graces is legitimate, we need to be careful about thinking of them in too linear and sequential a manner. The division of the Exercises into four 'Weeks' is for the guidance of the director – the one giving the Exercises. It does not always correspond exactly with what is happening in the soul of the retreatant. 'The wind [Spirit] blows where it chooses' (John 3:8). This is why experienced directors will try to follow their retreatant rather than insist that the retreatant follow the directives in the text slavishly. By the same token, when a retreatant prays for a particular grace, it should not be a surprise if they receive a different one. If this is true in the context of the Exercises, so too can it happen in ordinary life.

Furthermore, to understand Second Week graces as inspiring active service of others, and Third Week graces as inviting to passive suffering with Christ, is overly simplistic. Theoretically the distinction is justifiable, but existentially matters are more complicated. Had Ignatius found himself placed with the Jesus of the public life – preaching, teaching, healing – the vision of La Storta would undoubtedly be easier to understand. However, its outcome might not have been as far-reaching or profound in terms of *mystagogy* – Ignatius's continuing induction into the full mystery of Christ.

Second and Third Week graces are not totally distinct, even if – for pedagogical purposes – they are dealt with sequentially in the *Spiritual Exercises*. In reality, they interact with each other, and are even interfused in the life of a person who prays. They cannot be kept apart or lived separately. Activity alternates with, and even coalesces with passivity, success with failure, delight with pain, consolation with desolation. Any human life – including a life of Christian ministry such as Ignatius and the companions desired to undertake – embraces all these dimensions, often at the same time.

A further important point is that, carrying his cross along the road to Calvary, Jesus continues to obey the Father and serve humankind as much as – even more than – during his public life. If this is true of Jesus, so will it be true of Ignatius and his companions. They too will 'deny themselves and take up their cross and follow Jesus' (Matthew 16:24), but this cross-carrying will be integral to their ministry, not separate from it. Like Jesus, they will suffer in their activity and be fruitful in their passivity.

Ignatius as priest

An overlapping approach to La Storta sees the whole event in the light of Ignatius's priesthood. It was five months since his ordination in Venice. His first mass, although not yet arranged, was constantly on his mind. Throughout the journey he was receiving many spiritual illuminations; the most conspicuous of these concerned the Eucharist. His two priest-companions, Laínez and Favre, celebrated mass each day, with Ignatius serving and receiving communion.

It was precisely as priests that the companions, as a group committed to an evangelical life, were determined to offer themselves in service to the Pope. Priesthood was now at the heart of their corporate identity. When others referred to them as *preti riformati* – reformed priests – the companions did not object, recognising it as a true description. This term was used in Italy for priests who lived a simple, prayerful life and devoted themselves to the well-being of the people. They did not form a separate organisation – nonetheless, by their very presence in their parishes, they were de facto part of a broader movement of Catholic reform. The early companions, although not parish based, continued to be associated with this brand of non-polemical reform in the years following their arrival in Rome.[47]

47 By the end of the 1540s Jesuits had begun to be involved in more overtly anti-Protestant polemics. This change of approach was brought about by the experience of Jesuits working in Germany, where the Protestant Reformation was growing in strength.

Without taking the priesthood of Ignatius into account, we risk limiting our understanding of what happened at La Storta. In particular, the ecclesial dimension of the vision will be missed. For, once priesthood is involved, the Church is involved. Ignatius was fully aware of this. So, when he hears Jesus speaking the words, 'I want you to serve us', he intuitively understands this to mean *priestly* service within the *Church*.

This interpretation of La Storta is corroborated by the presence in the vision of Jesus carrying his cross. He is walking towards Calvary in order to surrender his life as a sacrifice for humankind. As we read at length in Hebrews, Jesus is the great high priest – superseding the Temple priesthood in Jerusalem – and offering his own blood in sacrifice.

> In the days of his flesh, Jesus offered up prayers and supplications, with loud cries and tears, to the one who was able to save him from death, and he was heard because of his reverent submission. Although he was a Son, he learned obedience through what he suffered; and having been made perfect, he became the source of eternal salvation for all who obey him, having been designated by God a high priest according to the order of Melchizedek. (Hebrews 5:7–10)

This is the same Jesus with whom Ignatius finds himself placed. Ordination had bestowed on him a share in the high priesthood of God's Son and La Storta confirms the closeness of their union. All this is made possible because Ignatius too, following Jesus, has an attitude of 'reverent submission'. Hence the deepest meaning of Ignatius's own vocation – his call to priesthood – is revealed to him in a dramatic way.

CHAPTER 6

Spiritual Diary:
Ignatius and the Trinity

In 1541 the composition of Constitutions for the recently approved Society of Jesus was entrusted by the early companions to Ignatius and Jean Codure. The latter, however, died within a couple of months and Ignatius was left on his own with the task. The period 1541–44 turned out to be a time of rapid expansion for the Society. Besides the administrative work involved in governance, Ignatius was engaged in many apostolic projects in Rome itself. All the while he was suffering from serious ill health. He had little time or energy to give to writing the Constitutions.

However, in 1544 there was some easing of work pressures as the Society settled into a period of consolidation. Ignatius took up the composition of the Constitutions more actively and chose to begin by examining the kind of poverty most appropriate for the Society. The central issue was whether a fixed income should be allowed for the sacristies of churches attached to professed houses (residences for Jesuits who had taken their final vows). Ignatius had been party to a decision taken by the early companions in 1541 that allowed such an income. However, he now had second thoughts on the matter and was leaning towards excluding such income entirely. As a result, in order to learn what God wanted, he began a discernment that lasted forty days.

Discernment log-book

The so-called *Spiritual Diary*, consisting of two fascicules, or copybooks, has been helpfully identified by Joseph Munitiz as *a discernment log-book.*[48] In it Ignatius recorded his inner experiences during prayer (and occasionally outside of prayer) throughout this period. Writing it, therefore, was integral to his discernment – his decision-making process on poverty – or what the *Spiritual Exercises* would call his election (169–189). Anyone facing a serious decision today would be encouraged by their spiritual director to keep similar notes or records. Therefore, some knowledge of the dynamic of the Exercises – especially of the election – is necessary in order to understand the *Diary*. This applies especially to the entries in the first copybook.[49]

Ignatius also realised that some of the experiences that he wrote about might need to be revisited, either during his current discernment or later. He encircled these passages in the text and then copied them onto two separate pieces of paper. These he carefully preserved and happily they have survived.

The insight that Ignatius was seeking in regard to the Society's poverty was not imparted to him through a self-authenticating illumination – a First Time experience, in the terminology of the Exercises (175). He had to find another approach. He began by composing a separate document, which is also extant, noting the pros and cons, as he saw them, in regard to the poverty issue. He kept these notes by his side during his prayer throughout this whole period. There are several references to them in the text. Here he was using what the Exercises call the 'First method of making a sound and good election' in the Third Time (177–183). But however much he applied his reasoning powers – prayerfully considering the pros and cons of the argument – this method also failed to produce a result that satisfied him. So he eventually turned for enlightenment to his experience of consolations and

---

48 *Inigo: Discernment Log-Book. The Spiritual Diary of Saint Ignatius Loyola,* edited and translated by Joseph A. Munitiz SJ. London: Inigo Enterprises (1987). This translation is used throughout the book.

49 The first copybook covers the period from 2 February to 12 March 1544 (discernment on poverty). The second covers 13 March 1544 to 27 February 1545.

desolations – what the Exercises name as the Second Time for making an election (176).

The difficulties encountered by Ignatius in this discernment form a large part of its value for us. He experienced much uncertainty and confusion – even about the method he should use. There is an intriguing parallel with the Deliberation of the First Fathers in 1539 – the communal discernment that led to a decision to found the Society of Jesus. There, too, the group seeking to discern was forced to change their method of discernment in midstream, as it were.[50] Ignatius, as he pondered the issue of poverty, was not saved by his accompanying mystical experiences from the messiness that many people know may be part of a discernment. Mystical prayer does not provide an automatic shortcut to good decision-making.

Echoes of the *Spiritual Exercises*

For those who have some familiarity with the *Spiritual Exercises*, a helpful way of reading the *Diary* is to be alert to resonances of the former text – echoes of its themes and teachings. The election, or decision-making process, is the most obvious echo – indeed much more than an echo. However, other resonances will also strike the careful reader and are worth noting.

> ➤ The preparatory prayer in each individual exercise expresses the pervasive *climate of desire* in the *Diary*. 'To ask God our Lord for the grace that all my intentions, actions, and operations may be ordered purely to the service and praise of the Divine Majesty' (46). This prayer is often seen as an encapsulation of the First Principle and Foundation (23).
> ➤ The *id quod volo* appears constantly in one form or other. It is described in the Exercises as 'to ask God our Lord for what I want and desire' (48). Ignatius's petitionary prayer in the *Diary* is sometimes specific (e.g. focused on the poverty

---

50 English translation in Jules J. Toner SJ, 'The Deliberation that Started the Jesuits: A Commentary on the *Deliberatio Primorum Patrum*'. *Studies in the Spirituality of Jesuits,* 6/4 (1974), 193–208.

question) and at others more open-ended (even praying for graces beyond his capacity to imagine or name). He has also learned that God, supremely free, may answer his petition in totally unexpected ways.

➤ In the Exercises, what is called 'a composition made by imagining the place'[51] is proposed as a way of grounding the attention of the person as they begin their prayer. It will vary according to the subject matter of each exercise. Ignatius explains what he means in some detail (47). Throughout the *Diary* a favoured composition of place for Ignatius is that of imagining himself before the heavenly court. This is the 'composition' recommended for the exercise on the Three Classes of Persons – 'Here it will be to imagine myself as standing before God and all his saints, that I may desire and know what will be more pleasing to the Divine Goodness' (151), and again for the Contemplation to Attain Love – 'Here it is to see myself as standing before God our Lord, and also before the angels and saints who are interceding for me' (232). This imaginative stance is consonant with the ethos of chivalry so central to Ignatius's cultural upbringing, and with his own youthful service at court. In the *Diary* it is used especially whenever there is a question of an offering of himself to God.

➤ Mediators play an important role in the *Diary*. In Chapter 5 we saw how Ignatius uses a Triple Colloquy in the Exercises – asking the same grace, first of Our Lady, then of her Son, and finally of the Father (147). However, the number of mediators in the *Diary* increases significantly in comparison with the Exercises. The following supplies a vivid example:

A little later I wondered where I should begin, and it occurred to me that it might be with all the Saints,

---

51 This terminology comes from the Spanish text. The shorter, more familiar form, 'composition of place', is found in the Latin versions.

putting my cause in their hands, so that they might pray to Our Lady and her Son to be intercessors on my behalf before the Blessed Trinity ... I set about repeating the past offerings, beseeching and nominating as intercessors on my behalf the Angels, the holy Fathers, the Apostles and Disciples, and all the Saints, that they might plead to Our Lady and her Son. (46)

➤ The influence of the Annotations (introductory explanations) in the Exercises can also be perceived. Annotation 2 reads: 'For what fills and satisfies the soul consists, not in knowing much, but in our understanding the realities profoundly and in savouring them interiorly *(el sentir y gustar de las cosas internamente).*' We recognise this principle at play in Ignatius throughout his discernment on poverty – and even more so whenever he leaves it aside. He simply stays with his experience in prayer, accepting it with gratitude and delighting in it. In spite of his having the document listing the pros and cons of the argument by his side, Ignatius records comparatively little cognitive activity in the *Diary.* New insights of a rational kind are infrequent, and those that do come are overwhelmingly revelations *de arriba* (from above) about the mystery of the Trinity.

➤ Also operative is Annotation 3 which reads:

> In regard to the affective acts which spring from the will we should note that when we are conversing with God our Lord or his saints vocally or mentally, greater reverence is demanded of us than when we are using the intellect or understanding.

This teaching refers especially to the colloquies which are to be made 'in the way one friend speaks to another, or a servant to one in authority' (54).

In the *Diary* it is evident that Ignatius is always seeking this attitude. Particularly helpful is to ponder his use of the terms 'submission' *(acatamiento)*, 'reverence' *(reverencia)* and 'humility' *(humildad)* whenever they occur either singly or conjoined. They become particularly prominent at the commencement of the second notebook. On 17 March he writes (my emphases):

> Tears before mass and during it, so many that at times I lost the power of speech. All this visitation had for object now one Person, now another, in the same way as the previous day, and with the same effect. It confirmed my previous experience with regard to the *submission* and *reverence*, viz. that I had found in these the way I was intended to see. I considered it the best of all ways that I could be shown and felt that I should follow it for ever ... Later, the Giver of Graces provided me with such an abundance of knowledge, visitation, and spiritual relish ... that every time I mentioned God, 'Dominus' etc., I seemed to be penetrated so deeply, with a *submission* and *reverent humility* so admirable, that they seem to defy description. (164)

➤ The person of Christ is omnipresent in the *Diary*, yet this presence is not as centre-stage as in the *Spiritual Exercises*. Ignatius does not appear to be making gospel contemplations during this period. When Christ is named explicitly in the *Diary* it is almost always in the context of his relationship with the Father and the Spirit – i.e. as the Second Person of the Trinity, or as mediator. Therefore, in comparing the spirituality of the two texts, it is not sufficient simply to count the number of explicit references to Christ. It is better to ask *how* Christ appears in the pages of the *Diary*, in what *circumstances*, and what *role* he is playing.

Throughout the *Exercises*, relating with Christ in his humanity is the starting point of a journey into the mystery of God. As Paul wrote, 'He is the image of the invisible God … For in him all the fullness of God was pleased to dwell' (Colossians 1:15; 19). We are encouraged to keep our eyes on the human Christ so that we may learn from him (Second Week), and ultimately become one with him (Third and Fourth Weeks).

Remarkably, the dynamic can sometimes be the reverse in the *Diary*. 'It seemed in some way to be from the Blessed Trinity that Jesus was shown or felt, and I remembered the time when the Father placed me with the Son' (67). Here Ignatius's first point of reference is the Trinity, and it is they who reveal Jesus – the enfleshed Word of God. The momentum is not leading from Jesus to the Trinity, but from the Trinity to Jesus. This development in Ignatius's prayer points to its increasingly mystical nature.

The reference to the vision of La Storta (see Chapter 5) makes a similar point – but more simply. It is the Father who places Ignatius with Christ – the Son. The Father, working through the hidden Spirit, is the main actor in the drama. Contrast this with the call-texts in the gospels where it is Jesus who is in the spotlight and who takes the initiative – inviting certain men to accompany him and share in his proclamation of the Kingdom.[52]

There is a *contrasting* echo of La Storta on 27 February. Here, instead of the Father placing Ignatius with Christ, Christ (acting as Ignatius's representative and mediator) places him with the Trinity. It is enlightening to notice how Ignatius describes the outcome of this vision: tears and love

---

52 'He went up the mountain and called to him those whom he wanted, and they came to him' (Mark 3:13).

towards Jesus; submission and reverential love towards the Trinity (see the earlier discussion of these latter terms).

> I entered the chapel and while praying felt, or to put it more exactly, I saw, not by natural power, the Blessed Trinity and also Jesus who was representing me, or placing me before the Trinity, or acting as mediator close to the Blessed Trinity, that I might communicate in that intellectual vision. On feeling and seeing in this way I was covered in tears and love, but with Jesus as the object; and toward the Blessed Trinity, a respect of submission more like a reverential love than anything else. (83)

More on the Trinity

A central thesis in this chapter is that the predominant place of Christ in the *Exercises* is taken by the Trinity in the *Diary*. There is dissimilarity as well as similarity between the spirituality of the two texts. It is not a new spirituality that emerges in the *Diary*, but one that has evolved – and evolved considerably – from that of the *Exercises* and the Manresa experiences that underpinned them (see Chapters 3 and 4). We recall the vision of the Trinity at Manresa, the intensity of Ignatius's response to it, and his assertion: 'This experience remained with him for the rest of his life so that whenever he prayed to the Most Holy Trinity he felt great devotion' (28). In spite of this, he gives little specific attention to the Trinity in the *Spiritual Exercises*.

The contemplation on the Incarnation furnishes the one exception (101–109). Here the image and narrative of the Three Persons gazing down on the suffering world give us not only our starting but the key for unlocking the entire mystery. However, apart from this contemplation, we generally find in the *Exercises* a more *implicit* presence of the Trinity – a presence not named or explained. For example, it is implicit in all the contemplations of the life of Jesus.

This is because his relationship with the Father is integral to his identity – 'The Father and I are one' (John 10:30), and because he has been anointed by the Holy Spirit – 'God anointed Jesus of Nazareth with the Holy Spirit and with power' (Acts 10:38). Wherever Jesus is, there too is the Father and the Spirit.

The Trinity is also present – implicitly rather than explicitly – in the Contemplation to Attain Love (230–237). Here the composition of place has the retreatant 'standing before God our Lord' (232). In Ignatius's writings this term usually denotes Christ. However, in the setting of the heavenly court ('also before the angels and saints') it is more likely meant to evoke *both* Christ *and* the Trinity. Similarly, the title 'the Divine Majesty', which occurs three times (233, 234, 235), probably has a Trinitarian as well as a Christocentric significance.

More subtly it might be argued that the theme of mutuality, underlined in the second introductory observation, suggests the Trinity: 'Love consists in a mutual communication between the two persons' (231). The inner life of the Trinity also consists in such a mutual communication – only in this case between three Divine Persons. Furthermore, the dynamic of mutuality between the divine and the human is found in all four points of the Contemplation. Hence, those making this exercise may find themselves inspired – even if subconsciously – to turn their attention to the mystery of the Trinity. Joseph Munitiz, approaching the matter from a different angle, reaches a similar conclusion:

In the *Diary*, an endearing phrase to refer to God is that of 'Giver of Graces': In the Contemplation [to Attain Love], a rough intimation of the treasures these words enclose is imparted. The gift is the Giver himself, a Giver who is both present and dynamic in the gift, a Giver who is infinite in the number and variety of his gifts, to such an extent that no gift is not the Giver himself. Here, in this notion of 'giving', of 'communication', which for Ignatius is the quintessence of love, is to be found the seed, hidden and expectant, of the trinitarian revelations.[53]

In Manresa, Ignatius had wondered about the propriety of praying to each Person of the Trinity individually, while also praying to the Trinity as such. Although he had dismissed this line of thought as a minor temptation, a disturbance of a similar kind appears in the *Diary* on 21 February. Here Ignatius addresses the matter with greater perceptiveness and theological depth.

Before, when I wanted to obtain devotion in the Blessed Trinity, I had not desired nor adapted myself to seek for it or find it when saying prayers to the Father, for I thought consolation and visitation would not occur then: but during this mass I knew or felt or saw, 'God knows',[54] that on speaking to the Father and seeing that He was One Person of the Blessed Trinity, I felt moved to love all the Trinity, especially as the other Persons were all in the Trinity by their very essence: the same feeling when I prayed to the Son and to the Holy Spirit; when I felt consolation I was delighted with any one of them, and I rejoiced in acknowledging it as coming from all three. So great an achievement did it seem to have untied this knot or accomplished something similar, that I could not stop repeating to myself, with reference to myself, 'Who are you? From where? etc. What did you deserve? Why this? etc.' (20)

Mass and early morning prayer
Many of Ignatius's Trinitarian visions are linked with the mass – occurring during his (often long) preparations beforehand, during the celebration itself, or during his thanksgiving afterwards.

53 *Discernment Log-Book*, 13.
54 Allusion to 2 Corinthians 12:2.

There is a certain theological coherence in this association of Trinitarian visions with the mass. Also noteworthy is that, of the 116 masses named in the *Diary*, thirty were masses of the Trinity. Ignatius had a regular self-imposed regime – centred on the mass – in the early morning. He followed it faithfully with few adaptations. Any changes that occurred came, not from external circumstances, but from modulations in his inner life – particularly in his desires. We will consider one particular entry – that of 4 March – in which he goes into some descriptive detail. This can serve to illustrate his normal practice. He had already decided, before rising that morning, to say a mass of the Trinity.

> When dressed, I looked at the Introit of the mass and felt all moved by great devotion and love directed towards the Blessed Trinity. Later, when I began the preparatory prayer before mass, I did not know to whom I should turn: first I attended to Jesus, and felt that He was not allowing Himself to be seen or felt clearly but in some sort of shadowy way difficult to see. Then as I attended, I felt that the Blessed Trinity allowed itself to be seen or felt more clearly or full of light. I began, and reasoned for a while with the divine Majesty. Suddenly the tears streamed down my face, I broke into sobs, and felt a love so intense that it seemed to unite me excessively close to Their own love, a thing full of light and sweetness. That intense visitation and love seemed quite remarkable and to surpass other visitations. Later when I entered the chapel, new devotion and tears, always directed to the Blessed Trinity: similarly, at the altar. Once vested, a far greater flood of tears, more sobs, and the most intense love, all for love of the Blessed Trinity. When I wanted to begin the Mass, I felt very great touches, and intense devotion to the Blessed Trinity. (32)

Ignatius intends his prayer to be on the Trinity, but has begun by turning first to Jesus as his mediator. However, Jesus seems somewhat withdrawn. It is only when the Trinity allows itself 'to be seen or felt' that Ignatius comes fully alive. Now he experiences an intensity of feeling and a great love – so much so that he feels united 'excessively close to Their own love'. Indeed, this intensity of feeling increases all the way through the account as Ignatius moves from his room to the chapel – then when he begins to vest and is about to say mass. We might notice too his use of three words that were a standard part of the medieval mystical vocabulary: 'devotion' and 'tears', which appear multiple times in the *Diary*, and 'touches', which appears more rarely.[55]

The Holy Spirit

As part of Ignatius's Trinitarian consciousness in the *Diary*, some of the most striking visions that he records are of the Third Person. The almost total absence of the Holy Spirit from the *Exercises* has often been commented on. There are a mere five references to the Spirit in the Mysteries of the Life of Christ (261–312), and one in the Rules for Thinking with the Church (365). Nothing more. But in the *Diary* such references are relatively frequent. Nine times Ignatius chooses to celebrate a Mass of the Holy Spirit. His choice of masses (when there is no liturgical feast occurring) is always significant because it reveals the focus of his desires on a particular day. On one of these occasions – 11 February – towards the end of his election on poverty, he records:

> During my customary prayer, without reconsidering the reasons for poverty, I offered it to God Our Lord ... I felt considerable devotion and tears. A little later I made a colloquy with the Holy Spirit, in preparation for saying His mass; I experienced the same devotion and tears, and seemed to see or feel Him in a dense clarity or in the colour of burning flame – a way quite strange to me – all of which confirmed me in my election ...

55 See also the passage on the Spiritual Senses in Chapter 1.

Ignatius uses colour to describe either the object seen in a vision or his own inner response to it. At times, such as in this entry, it is difficult to apply this distinction with any confidence. When he writes of seeing or feeling the Spirit 'in a dense clarity or in the colour of burning flame', is he describing how the Spirit appeared to him, or how he felt in the presence of the Spirit? This is the language of the spiritual senses. Since sense-knowledge – spiritual as well as physical – is a passive mode of knowing, perhaps the distinction does not matter. Is the green of the grass inherent in the grass itself, or is it solely in my eye?

> A little later, just before going out to say mass, while I prayed for a short while, I felt intense devotion and wept on feeling or seeing in some way the Holy Spirit – the question of the election being now answered – and I could neither see nor feel either of the other two Divine Persons in this way. (14–18)

His earlier colourful description of feeling or seeing the Holy Spirit has been replaced by the haziness of the phrase, 'in some way'. Yet he still experiences intense devotion and tears. He knows that he is seeing the Holy Spirit and is able to contrast this with his inability to see or feel the other two Persons of the Trinity.

Ignatius seems to have had to wait until later in his life for the Holy Spirit to become conspicuous in his spirituality. This is borne out by Laínez, who writes:

> He has told me several other things about the visitations he has had concerning the mysteries of the faith as, for example, about the Eucharist; especially about the person of the Father; and some time after that, I think, about the person of the Word; and lately *(últimamente)* about the person of the Holy Spirit.

Here we are offered a simplified – indeed overly schematic – sketch of Ignatius's spiritual enlightenment. The passage acknowledges – without attempting an explanation – the absence of the Holy Spirit in Ignatius's earlier 'visitations'. Laínez then continues: 'I remember that he would say to me that, in his situation now, in the things of God Our Lord, he felt more passive than active.'[56] This points to the mystical quality of Ignatius's prayer in his mature years – around the time of the *Diary*. It is interesting to ponder whether this passivity is due to – or at least linked with – his new-found but growing awareness of the presence and influence of the Holy Spirit within him.

Difficulties and opportunities

There is no doubt that the *Diary* is the most difficult of Ignatius's writings to understand. This is one of the reasons why it is not better known. The difficulty stems in part from its being an exceedingly private document, not addressed to any projected readership, but written solely for Ignatius's own perusal. This 'privacy' is well illustrated by the personal code that he uses in much of the second notebook – researchers can only make an educated guess as to its meaning. Yet it is this very 'privacy' that guarantees the authenticity of the document. Unlike the *Autobiography*, where questions can be asked about Ignatius's motivations, memory and the selectivity of his narrative, the *Diary* is the uncensored daily record 'for his eyes only' of what was happening to him in prayer.

A further difficulty arises from the content of the *Diary*. Ignatius is recording mystical encounters – mostly related to the Trinity – that lie outside the experience of most people. Yet Christian readers will recognise that they share the same faith with Ignatius, and that they express that faith through the same creeds and modes of worship. It would be an over-simplification to say that the difference between Ignatius and ourselves is simply one of intensity of feelings – yet there is a vein of truth in that assertion. We have all been baptised 'in the name of the Father, and of the Son, and of the Holy Spirit'. We are already living in the Trinity

56 Diego Laínez, *Letters*.

and the Trinity is living in us. Furthermore, even though 'now we see through a mirror, dimly' (1 Corinthians 13:12), we are likely to have received at least occasional intimations of this mystery along our spiritual journey. The *Diary* encourages us to pay attention to such intimations when they occur - it can thus be both an inspiration and a challenge.

CHAPTER 7

As Seen by His Critics:
Melchor Cano and the Inquisition

We have been reflecting on Ignatius's mystical experiences as recorded in his writings. These sources give us his own perspective on what was happening in his soul and his own interpretation of how God was dealing with him. His accounts are supplemented by some of his early companions. But there were many times when others saw things differently. After his return from pilgrimage to Jerusalem (1523), and when he began to study and simultaneously engage in apostolic ministry in Barcelona, Alcalá and Salamanca, he attracted the attention of the Inquisition.[57] His ministry consisted mostly of spiritual conversation, sometimes with individuals, at other times with groups. Suspicions arose about the orthodoxy of what he was teaching – he was imprisoned and questioned and his behaviour was investigated. While not found guilty of being unorthodox, he never fully satisfied his interrogators, who consequently placed restrictions on his activities. This led to his decision to move on, first from Alcalá to Salamanca, then from Salamanca to Paris – all university cities. He was determined that the Inquisition would not force him to abandon his studies or his outreach to people.

To some it may seem odd, if not perverse, to devote an entire chapter to the opinions of those who regarded Ignatius with suspicion, if not outright hostility. This reaction is all the more understandable since what his opponents were attacking was not

---

57 An institution set up to defend the orthodoxy of the Catholic faith. It existed in a number of countries but in Spain (1478–1834) had a particular reputation for ruthlessness and cruelty. The Dominicans, or Order of Preachers, were prominent in its ranks. It had the support of *los reyes católicos*, Ferdinand II of Aragon (1452–1516) and Isabella I of Castile (1451–1504) who, after their marriage, moulded Spain into a united monarchy.

limited to his apostolic activities. It included his claims about his own inner experiences – precisely what we have been exploring in this book. For them his spirituality verged on the heretical and his mysticism was false. Instead of ignoring such views, it can be helpful and enlightening to listen to them carefully. Their proponents were not ignorant or silly people – indeed some were well-respected theologians. Some may have been biased – but who among us is not? Most had valid concerns which they expressed forcefully. Can we let their views challenge us to reflect more deeply on our own preconceptions and conclusions? We may discover to our surprise that we owe these opponents of Ignatius a debt of gratitude.

Ignatius an *alumbrado*?

The Inquisition suspected that Ignatius was a follower of the movement known as *alumbradismo*, or The Way of Enlightenment.[58] A person associated with this movement was called an *alumbrado* (literally an Enlightened One). The term originated among opponents of the movement as a form of mockery, abuse and accusation. No individual or group ever claimed this name for themselves. Much of our knowledge of the early manifestations of *alumbradismo* (around the 1520s) comes from an 'edict of faith' issued by the Inquisitor General in 1525. It contained forty-eight propositions that were to be condemned. These were mainly statements attributed to members of the movement, or snatches of conversation overheard by hostile witnesses – hence they are to be treated with some reserve. The edict, in its own words, was directed against persons 'who call themselves enlightened, abandoned and perfect' (*alumbrados, dexados y perfectos*).

Many of the propositions in the 'edict of faith' express contempt for the cult of saints, the worship of images, indulgences, fasting, abstinence and the commandments of the Church. Others

---

58   Alistair Hamilton, *Heresy and Mysticism in Sixteenth-Century Spain: The Alumbrados.* Toronto: University of Toronto Press, 1992. I mostly rely on this work.

promote *dejamiento* – abandonment or a totally passive reliance on the divine will. If a person finds themselves in such an inner state, no special form of prayer is required. (This is, in part, a dismissive reference to liturgical prayer.) Furthermore, all activity is an obstacle to the divine presence in the soul. It is wrong to ask anything of God, to think about the humanity of Christ, or even to remember God deliberately. These opinions – in so far as they could justifiably be ascribed to the *alumbrados* – led to disdain for all tradition and authority.

There are good reasons for doubting if many people in Spain embraced such extreme views, and even better ones for doubting that those who did constituted an organised movement. *Alumbradismo* never had a formal leadership. However, the Inquisition, by and large, was convinced that the accusations in the 'edict of faith' were true and it acted accordingly. Its remit – to defend the purity of the Catholic faith – was understandable in the context of the time. However, its judges became obsessive in seeking out signs of heresy and often treated the accused as guilty unless proven innocent. In Spain they had three main targets – *alumbradismo*, Erasmianism (the teaching of the Dutch humanist, Desiderius Erasmus), and Lutheranism – all growing in influence at this time.

The reasons for the suspicion that fell on Ignatius were many. When he arrived in Alcalá in 1526, he became acquainted with some prominent individuals who were later pursued by the Inquisition on charges of *alumbradismo*. He chose one of them, the Portuguese priest, Manuel de Miona (c.1477–1567), as his confessor. In 1530 Miona had to flee Spain, became Ignatius's confessor for a second time in Paris, and later joined the Society of Jesus. Another cause for concern in Alcalá was the eccentric and suspicious manner in which Ignatius and his four young male companions chose to dress – in a long grey habit and grey hood.

Ignatius soon became the leader of a group of people who were looking for spiritual guidance. The majority of these were women. Here, too, there were some who were associated, even if only marginally, with the *alumbrados*. During their meetings some of the younger women became subject to seizures. Some broke out in sweat and fainted, some vomited, and some writhed on the ground, claiming to have visions of the devil. When these phenomena became more widely known, the Inquisition could hardly ignore them. In November of that year, Alonso Mejía, acting as the inquisitorial visitor in the University of Alcalá, began an investigation. This was to be the first of many.

Annotation 15

At the core of the different factors that troubled the Inquisition lay Ignatius's attitude to inner experience. He appeared convinced that God communicated directly with the individual person – just as the *alumbrados* believed. We saw in Chapter 3 how, after narrating his first four visions at Manresa, he had said in the *Autobiography*:

> These things that he saw at that time fortified him and gave such great support to his faith that many times he thought to himself: if there were no Scriptures to teach us these matters of faith, he would still resolve to die for them on the basis of what he had seen. (29)

This could, perhaps, be dismissed as simply rhetorical – an overly dramatised and exuberant reaction to his own personal experience. However, in Annotation 15 to the *Spiritual Exercises* he expresses a similar conviction in more temperate language. Now he is no longer speaking about himself, but is making a generalised statement, relevant to anyone making the Exercises.

> But while one is engaged in the Spiritual Exercises, it is more suitable and much better that the Creator and Lord in person communicate himself to the devout soul in quest of the divine will, that he inflame it with his love and praise, and dispose it for the way in which it could

better serve God in the future. Therefore, the director of the Exercises, as a balance at equilibrium, without leaning to one side or the other, should permit the Creator to deal directly with the creature, and the creature directly with his Creator and Lord. (15)

There is no doubt that this teaching has similarities to The Way of Enlightenment. However, unlike the *alumbrados*, Ignatius never draws the conclusion that, because inner experience of God can be real and can be trusted, there is therefore no need for the authority of the Church or the rituals of Christian worship. This nuanced stance is what protects Ignatius from heresy. In spite of – or, more correctly, because of – his mystical experiences at Manresa and later, he held to the necessity of remaining part of the incarnational reality of the Church, the Body of Christ.[59] A person's inner experience and the life and teaching of the Church are not in conflict with each other, rather they are polarities that need to be held in a healthy tension. Both communicate truth although in different ways. To deny or disparage one polarity at the expense of the other is to deprive oneself of an irreplaceable source of understanding and spiritual nourishment.

In other words, Ignatius believed that inner experience and church authority are not *alternative* sources of knowledge, truth, wisdom or even revelation. They are *complementary* sources which need to interact and dialogue with each other. Both have something important and distinctive to say, and both make their unique contribution to what Ignatius called discernment.[60] Here we recognise the valuable contribution he has made to the life and growth of the individual Christian – as well as to the life and growth of the Church.

59 See Michael J. Buckley, 'Ecclesial Mysticism in the *Spiritual Exercises* of Ignatius', *Theological Studies*, 56 (1995), 441–63.
60 For reading on discernment, a good starting point is David Lonsdale, *Dance to the Music of the Spirit: The Art of Discernment*. London: Darton, Longman & Todd, 1992.

At the Cardoner Ignatius had seen and grasped the interconnectedness of all truth (see Chapter 4). This fundamental insight underpins his determination to preserve the two polarities – inner experience and church life – as revelatory of God. Cardoner also lies behind The Rules for Thinking with the Church in the *Spiritual Exercises* (352–370). These rules or guidelines reflect inter alia his own experiences of being branded an *alumbrado* and – along with the more obvious context of the Reformation – make more sense when read in that light.

Melchor Cano and the *Censura*[61]

The suspicions of *alumbradismo* that fell on Ignatius personally, beginning in the 1520s, were extended over the years to the book of the *Spiritual Exercises* and eventually to the Society of Jesus. One of the most prominent and capable of these critics was the Dominican theologian, Melchor Cano (1509–1560). He was implacably hostile to the *alumbrados*. His views are detailed in his lengthy critique of Bartolomé de Carranza (1503–1576), a fellow Dominican who was Archbishop of Toledo and Primate of All Spain. Cano accused him of teaching the doctrines of *alumbradismo* and had him tried for heresy by the Inquisition. Carranza was found guilty and spent sixteen years in prison.

Cano's attacks on Ignatius and his teachings came later. What adds a certain piquancy to the story is that the two men had met on several occasions. On each, Cano had got the impression that Ignatius was lacking in integrity. Their first encounter occurred when Cano, happening to be in Rome, decided to pay Ignatius a visit. He was taken aback when his host, for no apparent reason, began to explain how he had been persecuted in Spain. Ignatius also recounted some revelations that he claimed to have received from God. From this behaviour, Cano judged that Ignatius was

---

61 Terence O'Reilly, 'Melchor Cano and the Spirituality of St. Ignatius Loyola: The *Censura y parecer contra el Instituto de los Padres Jesuitas*', in *The* Spiritual Exercises *of Saint Ignatius of Loyola: Contexts, Sources, Reception*. Leiden/Boston: Brill (2021), 227–57. This groundbreaking article is my main resource in writing on Cano.

vain and his revelations unworthy of credence. Their second and third encounters were also unsatisfactory so far as Cano was concerned. They left him with the conviction that Ignatius was ignorant of divine and human law, imprudent and indiscreet – as well as vain. His reputed holiness was more apparent than real.

Cano seems to have been building up his case against Ignatius over many years. Between 1556 and 1558 he wrote a number of letters in which he affirmed that the Society of Jesus was a heretical force whose Exercises were undermining both Church and state. He also wrote a more formal treatise around 1558 on these same lines with the intention of sending it to Pope Paul IV. This treatise was subsequently lost, and we do not know if the Pope ever received it. A document discovered in the British Library in 1977, attributed to Cano, is almost certainly the work in question. Its title reads: *Censura y parecer contra el Instituto de los Padres Jesuitas*, but it is more often referred to simply as the *Censura*.[62]

Cano's monograph is comprehensive and well-argued. What follows is a summary of the main lines of his critique of the *Spiritual Exercises*:

- Firstly, Cano deplores the fact that the Exercises make the same contemplative spirituality available to everybody – irrespective of different temperaments and callings. He believes that it is not possible to combine the active life with the contemplative life. Hence, he is concerned that people who try to do so may neglect the works proper to their God-given vocation. This, in his view, has been an error of the *alumbrados*. Some of the latter have been led, in their misplaced enthusiasm, to abandon their responsibilities to home, work and family. Cano fears that, through the Exercises, the same social and moral upheavals will occur and spread more widely.

---

62 Transcribed in O'Reilly, ibid., 248–57.

- Secondly, Cano disapproves of the importance that the Exercises accord to affective spiritual experience. Those making the Exercises, he writes, are given to understand that they will *experience* the work of grace in their soul and be granted consolations. To make such a promise is blatant presumption – an attempt to force or anticipate the hand of God. He also affirms that those making the Exercises are encouraged to describe in words the affective graces they have received – in this way edifying those who listen. In practice, he argues, this means that, during their meditations, they are not only nourishing themselves but also preparing nourishment for others. This is bound to leave their own souls unfulfilled.

- Thirdly, Cano criticises the advice given to a person during the Exercises to seek *indifference* as a means of discerning God's will. He is almost certainly identifying, or at least associating, Ignatian indifference with the *dejamiento* or abandonment promoted by the *alumbrados*. If so, he misunderstands what Ignatius means by indifference as, for example, in the First Principle and Foundation (23). Cano also argues that Jesuits have erred by according an excessive and distorted importance to conformity with the will of God. In his view, this is also an attitude that resembles the teaching of the *alumbrados*. These two major objections make Cano highly suspicious of the entire decision-making process in the Exercises – i.e. the election (169–89).

- Referring to what Ignatius says about God being allowed to work directly on the soul (Annotation 15 above), Cano calls it *una clausula no muy sana* – not a very wholesome teaching. He holds that this way of discerning God's will undermines respect for reason, learning and authority. This was also a central accusation against the *alumbrados*.[63]

---

63 Accusations, similar though not always identical to those of Cano, were made by his fellow Dominican and member of the Inquisition, Thomás Pedroche (d. 1569). He chaired a commission set up in 1553 to investigate the orthodoxy of the *Spiritual Exercises* and wrote up its negative report.

Similarities and differences

It would be easy to concentrate on Cano's exaggerations and blind spots, and so dismiss his critique as a witch-hunt and his arguments as irrelevant. However, this would be unwise. Yes, Ignatius was never an *alumbrado* nor do the *Exercises* promote *alumbradismo*. The judgments given at his various ecclesiastical trials confirm this. The very fact that some of these trials were held at Ignatius's own insistence shows that he respected Church authority and wanted his orthodoxy to be vindicated. His desire was to teach the faith of the Church from *within* the Church and as its representative – unlike the *alumbrados* who had isolated themselves on the periphery of the institution.

However, in order to take Cano seriously, it will be helpful to tease out further a number of the similarities between Ignatius and the *alumbrados*. In doing this, we will also become aware of their differences. We begin with a straightforward example: Ignatius and the *alumbrados* taught what is generically called mental prayer (meditation/contemplation). But rather than doing this in an exclusive way, Ignatius embraced and encouraged vocal prayer as well. Here he differed from the *alumbrados*, who were critical and dismissive of vocal prayer. At the beginning of the *Spiritual Exercises* we read:

> By the term Spiritual Exercises, we mean every method
> of examination of conscience, meditation, contemplation,
> vocal or mental prayer, and other spiritual activities, such
> as will be mentioned later. (1)

Ignatius does not establish a hierarchy within the different ways of praying, but encourages a person to discover the way that suits them best, or that seems most appropriate at a particular time. Compared with the *alumbrados* he is much less prescriptive. He is confident that God will work with whatever choice a person makes – indeed God will have guided them to that particular choice. All that matters is openness to God.

The *alumbrados* were also dismissive of the rituals and ceremonies – the external, corporate expressions – of Christian worship. Ignatius, on the other hand, engaged in them enthusiastically. He also defended such rituals against many of the Protestant reformers – as well as against the *alumbrados* – in the Rules for Thinking with the Church.

> We should praise frequent attendance at Mass; also, chants, psalmody, and long prayers inside and outside the church; and further, the schedules setting the times for the whole Divine Office, for prayers of every kind, and for all the canonical hours. (355)

Furthermore – an issue not mentioned by Cano – the prominence that Ignatius gives to the Passion in the *Spiritual Exercises* contrasts with the condemnation by the *alumbrados* of contemporary Spanish devotion to the Passion.

Further shared convictions

Among the beliefs, attitudes and aspirations shared by Ignatius and the *alumbrados*, three merit further exploration.

• Firstly, both Ignatius and the *alumbrados* were convinced of the possibility of combining contemplation and action. One consequence was that they both considered their teaching on prayer to be universal – relevant to all believers – and not of value only to those living some form of consecrated life. Erasmus was of a like mind. He had popularised his views on the call of the laity to holiness in his widely read *Enchiridion Militis Christiani* (Handbook of the Christian Soldier) in 1503. This convergence between the *alumbrados*, Erasmus and Ignatius might be called a sign of a growing democratisation of prayer and of the idea of holiness. Not surprisingly, all three were regarded with suspicion by the Inquisition.

- Secondly, Ignatius and the *alumbrados* expressed confidence in the possibility of an affective experience of God's love. Spirituality is a matter of the heart as much as of the mind – feelings *and* insights are important. God communicates with us through both channels. Ignatius found that the Spanish word *'sentir'* served to describe the coming together of the two in a single experience. He used it frequently to mean *a felt understanding*, or *a feeling permeating insight*. In this Ignatius and the *alumbrados* were in line with the medieval and Patristic teaching on prayer. It was their opponents who had departed from the earlier tradition, mistrusting affectivity and relying on an exaggerated rationality. This trust in affectivity – even as a way of experiencing God's love – was part of Ignatius's wider conviction about the validity of inner experience.

- Thirdly, Ignatius and the *alumbrados* believed in the possibility of divine guidance in the ordinary decisions of life. God is interested not only in our eternal salvation but in all our joys and sorrows, whether great or small – along with the ways in which we deal with them. In the Contemplation to Attain Love, Ignatius writes: 'I will consider how God dwells in creatures ... and how in this way he dwells also in myself' (235); 'I will consider how God labours and works for me ... he acts in the manner of one who is labouring' (236). God abides and is active in each of us – *personally* involved in everything that concerns us, even the trivial and the mundane.

Despite these striking similarities, however, we have already seen that the conclusions drawn from them by Ignatius and the *alumbrados* were completely different. This was notably the case in relation to authority – above all, Church authority. The *alumbrados* were known as rejecting it – or at least seeing it as irrelevant to themselves – while Ignatius acknowledged and submitted to it. As we argued earlier, he was happy to hold polarities in tension, however much they seemed to be pulling in opposite directions.

He did not need to eliminate one polarity in order to defend the other. Thus he had an equal respect for the authority of inner experience – his own and that of others – and for Church authority.

Returning to Cano

We have seen how Cano could have reached his negative judgements on Ignatius, given the similarities between the latter's teaching and certain aspects of *alumbradismo*. Cano, of course, was relying on less evidence than we have access to today. He based his conclusions on the *Spiritual Exercises* – the book itself and what he observed in those who made the Exercises – and to a lesser extent on his personal encounters with Ignatius. He did not have access to the *Autobiography*, which was dictated towards the end of Ignatius's life,[64] or to the *Spiritual Diary*, whose existence was known to Ignatius alone. These are now considered the key resources for understanding Ignatius's prayer-life and mysticism.

Would Cano have changed his opinion about Ignatius and the *Spiritual Exercises* if he had had the opportunity to study these other two documents – especially the *Spiritual Diary*? From what we learned about the *Diary's* contents in Chapter 6, such a volte-face seems highly unlikely. Indeed, he would have discovered even more evidence of what he regarded as *alumbradismo*, and little to convince him of the authenticity of Ignatius's mystical experiences. The three chief characteristics that Ignatius shared with the *alumbrados* are still present.

- Firstly, the combining of contemplation with action. Ignatius was living a very full and busy life during the period covered in the *Diary*. And although he mostly wrote about what was happening during his prayer and while celebrating mass, he also noted other incidents from outside of prayer that

---

64 Cano's attacks on the Society of Jesus and its spirituality continued after Ignatius's death. However, since the Society was extremely protective of the *Autobiography*, it is unlikely that Cano had access to it even then.

he considered worth remembering. God breaks in on him in the most ordinary of circumstances, in any kind of situation whatever.

> Today, even when walking in the city, I felt great interior joy, and on seeing three rational creatures together, or three animals, or three other things, the Blessed Trinity was brought before me: and so continuously. (55)

Later, as his discernment on poverty comes to an end (12 March), he receives the final confirmatory consolations, not during his prayer, but while he is having his midday meal. He even records the exact time: 'When I sat at table, after 19 hours had struck'.[65] Then, having described what happened within him during the meal, he ends:

> When I said grace after the meal, the Being of the Father partly disclosed itself, also the Being of the Blessed Trinity, while I felt a spiritual impulse moving to devotion and tears, such as I had not felt or seen all day, although I had often sought for it. Today's great visitations had no particular or distinct Person for their object, but in general, the Giver of Graces. (153)

- Secondly, the *Diary* is suffused with confidence in the affective, and even sensual, experience of God's love. Ignatius is constantly seeking such an intimate encounter with God and even gives the impression of expecting it to happen.
- Thirdly, the *Diary* conveys Ignatius's conviction that God can and does guide the Christian in the ordinary decisions of life. Of course, the issue of the poverty of the Society was not exactly ordinary, or a matter of small importance. But

---

65 In today's reckoning, 1.30 pm.

it is clear from the *Diary* that Ignatius was *always* aware of God's presence and enlightening help – no matter how minor or mundane the matter involved.

We can only conclude that if Cano had read the *Diary*, far from being reassured, he would have found his worst fears confirmed. The evidence that it provides would have reinforced that found in the *Spiritual Exercises*. Ignatius, in Cano's eyes, would again have shown all the signs of being an *alumbrado*.

Coda

Cano has often been painted as the villain of the story – an assessment that is unfair. He was a good man, a competent theologian and, like Ignatius, 'a man of the Church'. They were both working for ecclesial renewal at a time of great uncertainty. Cano's links with the Inquisition made him hyper-sensitive to anything that appeared to be heretical. It is worth stressing that Ignatius never took a stance against the Inquisition as such – he supported its aims even though he suffered from some of its methods.

As regards the spirituality promoted by Ignatius, Cano was sufficiently clear-sighted to be able to isolate its core elements. He did not attempt to distort or falsify the evidence – his interpretation was simply different from that of Ignatius. The two men disagreed in their understanding of God, and of the way in which God communicates with humans. Mystical experiences were quite 'normal' in Ignatius's view of the Christian life, while they were at best marginal – and mostly untrustworthy – for Cano. Ignatius brought to them a hermeneutic of generosity; Cano a hermeneutic of suspicion. We are in Cano's debt for contributing to this instructive dialogue.

Epilogue

The aim of this book has been to reflect on Ignatius Loyola as a mystic. We have mostly avoided tackling more wide-ranging questions about the nature of mysticism in general. However, we will conclude by offering some thoughts on an issue that is broader than the consideration of any one mystic, yet is likely to have crossed our minds as we reflected on Ignatius. That is the relationship of mysticism with spiritual growth and holiness.

Growth in the tradition

The classical paradigm of spiritual growth is that of a movement through purgation and illumination, leading ultimately into union. Its origin is often traced to Pseudo-Dionysius (late fifth to early sixth century), and was developed by writers such as St Bonaventure (1221–1274). It was part of the Christian spiritual tradition inherited by Ignatius, and is mirrored in the structure of the *Spiritual Exercises*.

This paradigm is still called on today, although it is usually complemented by newer insights from spirituality and psychology. One important lesson that we have learned is not to interpret it in a rigid and doctrinaire way. Particularly to be avoided is any tendency to understand it in a purely linear form – as if the components (purgation, illumination, union) inevitably follow one another in strict sequence. This would be misleading and disingenuous. The paradigm must be understood and applied flexibly and subtly. When approached in this manner, it will be found to offer many valuable insights into the dynamics of spiritual growth. However, it remains a theory – not a programme to be implemented, and certainly not a blueprint for life.

Purgation, illumination and union are often referred to as *stages* in spiritual growth. This may not be the most helpful terminology – even though it is not totally wrong. It is also possible to speak of inner *spaces* that we inhabit – at one point finding ourselves being purified (in a purgative space), at another being enlightened (in an illuminative space), at another being drawn into union with God (in a unitive space). Indeed, these spaces can overlap, making it possible to be in more than one space at the same time.

The clarity and coherence of the classical paradigm enables us to comprehend spiritual growth at the *notional* level. However, to grasp the dynamic of growth at the *existential* level, we need to give equal attention to our own and other people's experience. Once we have closely observed this existential dynamic, we can then turn to, and dialogue with, the classical paradigm and the interpretive writing that has grown up around it.

Towards union

Where does spiritual growth lead? Is it a movement towards the fulfilment of our deepest human desire? There is a near-consensus across the world faiths that our destined goal is union with Ultimate Reality – God (or however this Reality is named in the different traditions). Christians believe that the definitive fulfilment of this growth (and desire) is reached in heaven. But what about union with God on this side of the grave? Is it possible? If it is, what form does it take? Can we be conscious of it, or does it take place within the unconscious? Is there anything we can do to prepare for it? Or is it a pure gift from God – independent of our level of integrity, holiness or prayer?

The Greek philosophical tradition contributed greatly to Christian reflection on the desire for union and the nature of that union. This is especially true of the Neo-Platonic school of thought which was the seedbed for the growth-paradigm of Pseudo-Dionysius. Neo-Platonists, with Plotinus (204/205–270) as their most exceptional teacher, held that intellectual union with the One was the peak of contemplation – the end point in which the journey of ascent climaxed.

During the Patristic period this philosophical teaching was adapted by many Christian theologians, both eastern and western. They spoke of union – still conceived of as intellectual – with the God who was made manifest in Christ. As this tradition evolved over coming centuries, it proved sufficiently accommodating to allow for other modalities of union – affective (as in the Cistercian and Franciscan traditions) and conative (a union of wills – as in the Ignatian tradition).

Conative union makes us one with God's lovingly salvific will for humankind. Paul wrote: 'God our Saviour, who desires everyone to be saved and to come to the knowledge of the truth' (1 Timothy 2:4). That desire of God becomes our desire too – totally and unequivocally. We want what God wants – and *only* what God wants. We become one with God in our desiring. For this reason, conative union is sometimes called a mysticism of service – such as was experienced by Ignatius at La Storta when he was placed with the Son (see Chapter 5). More broadly, its essence is implicitly present in the desire voiced in the Our Father: 'Your will be done, on earth as it is in heaven' (Matthew 6:10).

In the Jesuit Constitutions, conative union, or a mysticism of service, is elucidated by the image of the *instrumentum coniunctum cum Deo* – the (human) instrument conjoined (intimately connected) with God.

> For the preservation and development not only of the body or exterior of the Society but also of its spirit, and for the attainment of the objective it seeks, which is to aid souls to reach their ultimate and supernatural end, the means which unite the human instrument with God and so dispose it that it may be wielded dexterously by his divine hand are more effective than those which equip it in relation to human beings. (813)[66]

---

66 *The Constitutions of the Society of Jesus*, translated with an Introduction and Commentary by George E. Ganss SJ. St Louis, MO: Institute of Jesuit Sources, 1970, 332.

It is essential not to regard the three kinds of union as entirely distinct from each other. Nobody ever has an *exclusively* intellectual, affective or conative experience of God. Union necessarily involves the whole person – not some one single dimension of that person. Nevertheless, the three descriptive adjectives helpfully underline the *dominant* component in each case. They also serve to alert us to the range of the human experience of God.

The Life of Prayer

Our prayer-life – whether deemed mystical or not – never stands still but is constantly changing, constantly in movement. Hence the need to discern the *direction* of this movement over time. This is subtly different from trying to *measure* our progress. In the Christian tradition we are taught to look for certain signs of positive spiritual growth, among them: prayer is moving from activity to passivity, from complexity to simplicity, from wordiness to silence.

A person beginning their inner journey is usually *active*, even busy, during their prayer – reading, reflecting, working things out, gaining and applying new insights. Prayer is experienced as quite a *complex* matter, like putting together an intricate jigsaw. It is a challenge to get it right. The beginner also tends to have a lot to say to God, to lean towards *loquaciousness* – whether they are employing set prayer formulas (prayers composed by others), or verbalising their own thoughts and feelings. Their prayer may, in fact, be more self-centred than God-centred – although they are probably unaware of this. In some such way a normal prayer journey begins. However, the person who perseveres – ideally with the support of a spiritual guide or director – will soon move on.

This moving on will be towards what we have called *passivity, simplicity, silence*. Notice that these mature qualities are the exact opposites of those normally found in the beginner. A commitment to regular prayer teaches a person that there is no need to be constantly active. Another actor is at work – the Spirit of the creator God. Let him/her take the initiative. Similarly, time teaches that prayer is not a puzzle to be solved and that there is no such thing as 'getting it right'. It is *we* who make prayer complex. There is no need for us to talk so much, 'to heap up empty phrases as the Gentiles do' (Matthew 6:7). Prayer is an invitation to listen, to be quietly attentive, and to move more and more into deep silence. Eventually the person may be able to rest, more or less habitually, in that silence 'like a child in its mother's arms, as content as a child that has been weaned' (Psalm 130:2).

Mysticism, growth and holiness

At this point, we do well to revisit some aspects of what we mean by the term mysticism. In Chapter 1, we saw that it is possible to distinguish two kinds of mysticism: a) ordinary, everyday mysticism – the conscious, intentional living out of our baptismal graces; and b) extraordinary mysticism – which is marked by a greater intensity and sometimes by paranormal experiences. While ordinary mysticism is open to all Christians, extraordinary mysticism is a gift offered to a chosen few. Our question is: Is a mystic – of the extraordinary kind such as Ignatius Loyola – inevitably further along the path of holiness (or a life of virtue) than a more ordinary, faithful and prayerful Christian – an everyday mystic?

A crucial principle that can be overlooked in this discussion is that *holiness has precedence over mystical experience*. We can give an account of holiness – either in theory or in the concrete life of an individual – without any reference to (extraordinary) mysticism. There are some saints who have been recognised as mystics, and others who have not. One group is not regarded as more worthy of admiration than the other – there is no hierarchy among them. Their common characteristic is their holiness – because of which they were canonised.

Even though mysticism cannot be identified with holiness – and is not a prerequisite for it – can it be said to contribute to holiness? Does it still help? Would Ignatius have reached the same level of holiness without his (extraordinary) mystical experiences in Manresa, La Storta and Rome? These experiences certainly influenced his decisions, as we have seen throughout this book. These decisions, in turn, led him into a life of virtue – specifically into one of ecclesial service. Would he have taken that path in any case – even if God had been guiding him by more ordinary means?

It may sound anticlimactic to say that most of these questions are unanswerable. How could it be otherwise? Not only mystical experience, but holiness, too, is God's work in us. Neither is the outcome of our own efforts or *ascesis*. But God is invisible, intangible and profoundly mysterious. Hence, most Christians live in some kind of spiritual nescience. They learn to be content with *intimations* of God's involvement in their lives. Such intimations, even at their strongest, yield partial rather than comprehensive understanding.

Perhaps all that can be said is that extraordinary mysticism contributes to a person's holiness *if that is part of God's plan*. It then takes its place within that complex of aids available to all believers – alongside the wisdom of the Bible, the spiritual fecundity of the sacraments, the witness of other Christians, the richness of human relationships, the beauty of the universe and the joy of human creativity. As Paul said, 'We know that all things work together for good for those who love God, who are called according to his purpose' (Romans 8:28). Every human experience, from the most pedestrian to the most exalted, can be a stepping stone on the journey into holiness.

Select Bibliography

Comerford, Brendan, SJ, *The Pilgrim's Story: The Life and Spirituality of St Ignatius Loyola*. Dublin: Messenger Publications, 2017.

Eaglestone, Alexander, and Munitiz Joseph A., SJ, *Remembering Iñigo: Glimpses of the Life of Saint Ignatius of Loyola. The* Memoriale *of Luís Gonçalves da Câmara.* Translated with introduction, notes and indices. St Louis, MO: Institute of Jesuit Sources, 2004.

Egan, Harvey D., SJ, *Ignatius Loyola the Mystic.* Wilmington, DE: Michael Glazier, 1987. The latest edition comes from the publishers Wipf and Stock, Eugene, OR, 2020.

Ganss, George E., SJ, *The Constitutions of the Society of Jesus*, translated with an Introduction and Commentary. St Louis, MO: Institute of Jesuit Sources, 1970, 332.

Ganss, George E., SJ, *The Spiritual Exercises of Saint Ignatius*. A Translation and Commentary. Chicago, IL: Loyola University Press, 1992

Gavrilyuk, Paul L., and Coakley, Sarah (eds), *The Spiritual Senses: Perceiving God in Western Christianity*. Cambridge: Cambridge University Press, 2012.

Guigo II, *The Ladder of Monks and Twelve Meditations*, Kalamazoo, MI: Cistercian Publications, 1981.

Hamilton, Alistair, *Heresy and Mysticism in Sixteenth-Century Spain: The Alumbrados.* Toronto: University of Toronto Press, 1992.

Julian of Norwich, *Revelations of Divine Love*, trans. Elizabeth Spearing, London: Penguin Classics, 1998,

Kavanaugh, Kieran, OCD (trans.), and Rodriguez, Otilio, OCD, *The Collected Works of St. John of the Cross.* Washington, DC: ICS Publications, 1991.

Laínez, Diego, and Polanco, Juan, *The First Biographies of St Ignatius Loyola.* Translated and edited by Joseph A. Munitiz SJ. Oxford: Way Books, 2019.

Lonsdale, David, *Dance to the Music of the Spirit: The Art of Discernment.* London: Darton, Longman & Todd, 1992.

Munitiz Joseph A., SJ (ed. and trans.), *Inigo: Discernment Log-Book. The Spiritual Diary of Saint Ignatius Loyola*. London: Inigo Enterprises (1987).

Palmer, Martin E., SJ, Padberg, John W., SJ, and McCarthy, John L., SJ (trans), *Ignatius of Loyola: Letters and Instructions*. St Louis, MO: Institute of Jesuit Sources, 2006.

Tylends, Joseph N., SJ, *A Pilgrim's Journey: The Autobiography of Ignatius of Loyola*. A translation and commentary. San Francisco, CA: Ignatius Press (revised edition 2001).

Von Hügel, Friedrich, *The Mystical Element of Religion as Studied in Saint Catherine of Genoa and her Friends*. Aeterna Press, 1909/2015.